GROWING UP WITH CHICO

GROWING UP WITH CHICO

★

MAXINE MARX

Prentice-Hall, Inc., Englewood Cliffs, New Jersey

Photo from Metro-Goldwyn-Mayer reprinted by permission. ©1935 Metro-Goldwyn-Mayer Corporation. Copyright renewed 1963 by Metro-Goldwvn-Mayer Inc.

Growing Up With Chico by Maxine Marx

Address inquiries to Prentice-Hall, Inc., Englewood Cliffs, N.J.   07632
Printed in the United States of America
Prentice-Hall International, Inc., London
Prentice-Hall of Australia, Pty. Ltd., Sydney
Prentice-Hall of Canada, Ltd., Toronto
Prentice-Hall of India Private Ltd., New Delhi
Prentice-Hall of Japan, Inc., Tokyo
Prentice-Hall of Southeast Asia Pte. Ltd., Singapore
Whitehall Books Limited, Wellington, New Zealand
10 9 8 7 6 5 4 3 2 1

Library of Congress Cataloging in Publication Data

Marx, Maxine.
   Growing up with Chico.
   Includes index.
   1.   Marx, Chico, 1887-1961.   2.   Marx Brothers.
3.   Comedians—United States—Biography.
4.   Moving-picture actors and actresses—United States—Biography.   I.   Title.
PN2287.M526M37   791.43'028'0924   [B]
ISBN 0-13-367821-0   80-15387

To my mother, Betty; my sons, Brian and Kevin; and most of all to the memory of my father, Chico.

Brian Marx Culhane, my son, was the greatest contributor to the completion of this book—without his help I never would have finished it. I would also like to thank Paul Wesolowski for certain factual data he supplied to me, Hector Arce for all his wonderful help, Phyllis Korper who sustained me in many dark hours, Elaine Hyman, steadfast and true, and Esther Margolis for her inspiration and guidance.

CONTENTS

PROLOGUE

Hollywood had never seemed more lush and tranquil. I finished my slow thirty laps in the pool's clear water, toweled off, and walked over to sit beside the gaunt, gray-mustached, deeply suntanned man sipping ice tea. It was a rare interval alone with him, on a day like so many others which brought admirers and friends to bask in the aura of this eighty-plus-year-old legend.

In some ways, I hated to disturb his peace.

"Groucho," I said, "there's something I have to get off my chest."

"Not your bathing suit by any chance?" Then the famous leer.

It felt like the old days: He was totally in control. I laughed self-consciously. "No . . . It's about a book I just finished reading. The one about you, Harpo, and Daddy."

For a few seconds, I heard only the faint lapping of the pool water against the gutters. Groucho's rheumy eyes widened slowly.

"That damn book!" Groucho spat.

Bravely, I pushed on. "How did all that dirt on Daddy get in there? I heard that the author taped some stuff with you."

My question was deliberately leading. I knew very well that the author had taped many of Groucho's reminiscences.

"Honestly, Maxine, I didn't know that guy would print all those things. Besides, you know, half the time I was just kidding around with him." His eyes drifted to the house that he had newly furnished.

"I want you to know that I'm very upset, Grouch. That book wasn't kind toward Daddy. It wasn't what you felt— You didn't dislike him or anything."

"What! I loved Chico!" Groucho said indignantly "Sure, he gave me plenty of cause to be angry sometimes. He fucked up, blew his brains and his money. . . . All Harp and I could do was stand by and watch. He wouldn't listen to us."

"Well, I think it's still a shame, Groucho. Daddy didn't deserve that book."

"I tried to stop the book from being published. Went to court. The guy took advantage."

I suddenly realized that the contents of the book had come as a shock to my uncle, even if he had given most of the information to the author himself. Groucho was old and sick, and his casual putdowns of my father had become so much of a habit that he hadn't really known how bad they would look in print.

I looked at Groucho. What did I expect to gain from belaboring the issue? At this late stage, it was hardly the time to begin hurling accusations. I just hoped that he would have less to say to the next researcher.

"Thanks for letting me use the pool, Uncle Groucho. It's so lovely here."

The last of the team that had shaped so much of my life looked almost benevolent in the midmorning California sun.

"Anytime, kid," he growled, not meeting my gaze.

The Marx Brothers were raised in a strange mixture of humor and poverty, stability, and continuous uproar. Frenchy, their father, made his living as a tailor. Actually, Frenchy was a terrible businessman, a lousy tailor, and most of his customers were one-time-only. But he was more than the handsome *schlemiel* that his sons later made him out to be. In his youth, Frenchy had been a fine dancer and a real ladies' man. He was also a fantastic cook. Unfortunately, his sons refused to acknowledge his authority, and as soon as he came home from work he would retire gracefully to the kitchen.

Minnie, my grandmother, was perfectly suited to play the lead role in the Marx household, and so her husband's withdrawal to the stove did not bother her in the least. She knew how to subdue her brood. Minnie was a great manipulator, a natural charmer who never wasted her time talking sense to her children when she could win them over by less straightforward means. When Shelley Winters played Minnie on Broadway in *Minnie's Boys*, I was struck by how well she captured Minnie's flamboyance and theatricality. The big blonde wig always slightly askew, the thick pancake makeup, the twin smears of rouge, and her long, trailing cheap gowns

1

made her look like a slightly tipsy Noh player. Minnie loved to be the center of attention, and the house was stocked with an assortment of admiring members of her family, the Schoenbergs. She so impressed everyone with her talents that she had them thinking she considered it a privilege to do the housework at the apartment on East Ninety-third Street, in the Yorkville section of New York City. Placing her one good ear against a pillow to shut out the noises of tenement life, Minnie would catnap most of the day in order to be fresh for the evening's songs, skits, and wicked impersonations.

The languages of New York City were echoed in the Marx home: German, some French, and the inevitable New Yorkese. It was a house loud with laughter, rich with the aroma of huge Alsatian meals whipped up by Frenchy, and crammed with a large family. The four brothers, Leonard (Chico), Adolph (Harpo), Julius (Groucho), and Milton (Gummo), in order of appearance at birth, shared one large double bed. (Zeppo had yet to be born.)

Chico (it rhymes with Chick, not Cheek) was his mother's favorite. Frenchy and Minnie's first baby, Manfred, died of tuberculosis, and when Chico was born in August 1887 he was showered with their frustrated love. Unlike Groucho, whom Minnie dubbed derisively *Der Eifersüchtige* (the jealous one), Chico mirrored his mother's German looks. He was very much the blond, blue-eyed child she had yearned for. Groucho was dark and dour, and spent most of his childhood picking up the crumbs of her affection.

All the brothers that followed in Chico's wake would feel that the eldest had forever captured their mother's heart. Perhaps as a result, Chico possessed less of an underlying coldness than his four brothers. He was, as Harpo once said, easily if not deeply moved. Graced with a whimsical, endearing manner, and a crooked, contagious smile (which he was always quick to brandish at the slightest provocation), throughout his life Daddy was an optimist. His laughter was explosive and unfeigned, not grudging like Groucho's, and he could laugh at himself, something his other brothers envied.

Chico treated everyone, even those he was giving short shrift to, with a great and sincere sweetness. He could display

2

a quality which only the Yiddish word *schmeikel* can describe: a charm based on the need to be adored, but nevertheless one that is quite endearing. Although he inherited these qualities from his mother, he was always his own man. Unfortunately, his "street smarts" developed rapidly, and by the age of nine Chico had become a compulsive gambler. By the time he was eleven, he was staying out all night with a tough neighborhood gang, spending his time hustling pool and getting into fights.

Frenchy found it impossible to stop his son's nightly ventures—he was all threat and bluster, with very little follow-through. His feeble whisk-broom spankings hurt Frenchy more than they did his sons.

Chico could have easily become a hard-core delinquent and ended up in prison or on Death Row, like many of his childhood buddies. But luckily he was too much of a coward (or too smart) to carry a weapon, something that his friends did as a matter of course.

I often wonder what would have happened if my father had continued his schooling. While in grammar school (the extent of his formal education), he amazed teachers with his aptitude for mathematics. His skill with numbers served him in later life not only as a gambler juggling odds, but as the eventual manager of the Marx Brothers' act.

In 1899 at his first job, Chico was in charge of maintaining the work records of his fellow employees at a lace factory. The job paid well enough, but it offered even greater rewards: The premises of the building held a floating crap game—and Daddy, aged twelve, became one of its permanent fixtures. Floating was a necessity since one of the factory's owners had a Puritan's loathing of gambling. "Absolutely No Gambling!" was posted throughout the building.

One day, after having made seven passes in a row, Chico was caught in the act by the anti-gambling partner of the factory and warned. Needless to say, the warning was less upsetting than the fact that all the money in the pot, which was rightfully Chico's, had disappeared while he was being bawled out.

Ten minutes later, after a brief work break, Chico followed the crap game into the men's room. Just as he was getting hot again, the same partner noticed Chico missing from his desk. He found him on the floor of the men's room, kneeling on a blanket, with a pair of dice in one hand. The others in the game had disappeared, although the bathroom's stalls did seem unusually crowded.

"You've had your last warning," the partner snarled. "Collect your pay and get out!"

Chico collected the few dollars he had coming from the paymaster. Before he could leave the building, he met the second partner of the factory, the one who had hired him because of his ability with numbers.

"Isn't it a little early to be leaving, Lenny?" the man asked.

"I was just fired," Chico replied disconsolately.

"That's nonsense," he was told. "Back to work."

A few minutes later, the first partner found Chico back at the same desk he had recently vacated.

"What are you doing here? I told you to leave, and I mean it!"

He scribbled a note and handed it to Chico. "Give this to the paymaster."

Once again, Chico presented himself to the paymaster, who shrugged as he counted out Chico's money.

As Chico was leaving for the second time, he again ran into the friendlier partner, who put his arm around the boy's shoulder and personally escorted him back to his desk.

Chico had barely settled down when the first partner returned.

"I've had just enough of this!" he bellowed. "Now you come with me."

Chico was dragged to the paymaster. "I want you to give this fellow one week's pay and that's it."

"But . . . ," the paymaster protested.

"Pay him off!"

4

Chico got still more money. His former employer then took him to the door and shoved him onto the sidewalk, snarling, "And don't come back!"

Chico decided it had been a pretty good day. Minnie would be more than pleased. On too many occasions, coming home from other jobs, he would pass a pool hall and wind up losing his salary. This time, he planned to go directly home and hand her the money.

No such luck. On his way to East Ninety-third Street, he happened to pass a crap game.

Like many gamblers before and after him, Chico developed an odd set of morals which lasted him throughout his life. He never refused to pay a gambling debt (something which caused my mother endless grief), and he never forgave a welcher. Yet even as a young boy, he began to fashion elaborate lies to cover his obsession with cards, pool, and dice.

Getting a brief job in a company that produced paper goods, Chico succeeded in losing two weeks' salary in a mere two days. For the rest of that week, Chico hedged on how much he was making.

"Lenny," Minnie warned him, "you've got to stop this fooling around. I want you to bring home your salary and hand it over to me before you get a chance to waste it."

The end of the week rolled around and no Chico.

Dinner time passed, and Minnie and Frenchy were sure he was out on some street corner losing his pay.

They were startled by a loud knock at the door. Minnie opened it and let out a gasp. There was Chico, standing beside a mountain of toilet paper. For days he had smuggled out the paper from the factory roll by roll—hiding the loot in a friend's closet. Now he proudly explained to his family that as a reward for his hard work the boss had let him take his pay out in produce. His parents decided not to press the issue. Better something than nothing.

Frenchy and Minnie did not know what to do about their oldest boy. They couldn't force him to hold onto a job, and though he lost all of his money gambling, they couldn't stay angry at such a charmer for long. Minnie thought that a healthy alternative to Chico's gambling habit would be to direct his impulsive fingers elsewhere, so the family bought a beat-up secondhand upright piano. A Viennese piano teacher was hired at twenty-five cents a week to teach him the popular songs of the day. Unfortunately, she only taught her pupils to use their right hands, since she herself could only fake the left. Chico caught on quickly and unlike his teacher he managed to teach his left hand to do more than pick up rudimentary chords.

But his gambling ways were firmly entrenched, and it was inevitable that sooner or later he would choose to spend his waking and sleeping hours on the street. When, in his mid-teens, his parents were understandably unsympathetic with his desire to become a pool hustler, Chico flew the coop.

From then on, Chico might drop in on the Marx household for a few weeks at a time, but he was clearly more at home away from home.

The piano lessons began to pay off: Chico was able to get paying jobs in nickelodeons, and later on he would be doing the same work in a series of whorehouses, no doubt exchanging his services for those of the ladies'. His talent *was* pretty special. He could sight-read any piece of music and immediately transpose it into the key of C. He had a vast repertoire and could effortlessly come up with the right kind of song for the occasion. Many a boisterous client was subdued by a sentimental ditty.

But Chico never liked staying in one place or one job for too long. When he tired of a particular nickelodeon, he would hand his piano stool over to Harpo. The boss wouldn't realize the switch at first because the two brothers were dead ringers for one another. Harpo's repertoire, though, usually wasn't up to the demands of the job, consisting only of two songs, "Waltz Me Around Again, Willie!" and "Love Me and the World Is Mine." It wouldn't be long before he was given his walking papers, and the brothers were off for another theater. They had gone through just about every nickelodeon and fly-by-night joint in New York when Chico gamely decided that he would head on alone for New Jersey.

Daddy loved to romanticize his childhood years on the road, but in reality his school of hard knocks was a series of dumps in which he played a few old standards and then hoped the clientele would get drunk enough so he could sneak off somewhere and lay a bet. He may not have known the name of the town he was in, but the odds were good he knew what horses were running in the third.

Once in Atlantic City he bumped into a cousin who owned an oyster bar on the boardwalk. Chico had gone hungry for a few days while looking for a job, and when the cousin offered him lunch he eagerly stuffed himself with about seven dozen oysters. When telling this story, Daddy would typically forget to mention that he had almost died from the shock to his system. Finding Chico violently retching under the boardwalk, his cousin handed him a couple of bucks and made him promise never to come back.

Small and wiry, Chico was toughened by his experiences on the road. Still in his teens, he worked as a professional wrestler, touring with a small circus troupe for a while. After betting all his earnings on himself and losing, he switched to prize-fighting and boxed as a flyweight. Having won a series of bouts, he began to get cocky, and started thinking along the lines of a world championship. This idea was knocked into oblivion when he was K.O.'d by a lightly regarded opponent. What kind of sport is this?, he wondered. From that point on, he never saw the inside of a ring again, but for years after he was willing to wager tens of thousands of dollars at ringside.

About the time Chico was trying to make his way in the world, a girl was born to Max and Sarah Karp in a shabby tenement on Manhattan's Lower East Side. The birth was not an easy one. Their first child, George, had been born in Russia a few years earlier, after which Sarah's father forced Max to marry her. As soon as he could, Max bought passage to America, leaving behind his bride and son. An immigration official shortened his now-forgotten Russian name, and from then on the often-estranged family was simply "Karp."

Meanwhile, the outraged villagers back home collected enough money to send Sarah and George by steerage to New York, where Sarah planned to enlist the aid of her sister in locating her miserable husband. She did find Max, who, after pleading innocence, got her pregnant again, only to disappear forever.

Sarah gave birth to a girl, Betty, and stayed in America, living from hand to mouth for four years, never venturing beyond the world of Hester Street's Russian-Jewish community. Finally she gave up and set out for her homeland.

Too young to grasp the significance of moving across half the world, Betty clung to the familiar form of Sarah. For three weeks, all they ate was herring and cold potatoes as Sarah kept kosher, staying below deck with hundreds of other returning immigrants.

Back in Russia, undeterred by her first marriage, Sarah married again, this time to a man who ran the dairy concession on a nobleman's estate. Betty, my mother, spent her early childhood roaming the wooded estate or collecting animal bones with her friends to sell to the glue-maker in the village. But when Sarah's second husband died, leaving her a small inheritance, she decided to take her children back to America.

She got a job doing piecework for a tailor, but it wasn't enough. Finally, to support her family, Sarah had to send Betty and George to live with her sister on the Lower East Side. She knew their only chance in America was to get an education; it was either that or work twelve hours a day in a sweatshop.

Betty felt that she had been abandoned. But on those sleepless nights spent on a bed that consisted of two kitchen chairs, she made up her mind not to cry. She was a fighter. Once, after a teacher teased her about her heavy Russian accent, she got in the habit of walking down the street endlessly repeating "the" until she got the *th* right. She emerged from the poverty and instability of her childhood a high-spirited girl, and remained a giggler, quick to laugh at life's absurdities.

It was one thing she had in common with her future husband.

By 1907, Chico, a brash twenty-year-old, had settled in Pittsburgh. He had gotten a job with a song publishing firm, Shapiro, Bernstein & Co. of Philadelphia, and had proved so capable that he had been transferred to manage the company's other Pennsylvania branch.

Since it wasn't his nature to stay in one place for long, Chico soon found Pittsburgh palling. He convinced his assistant, Arthur Gordon, a handsome teen-ager with a beautiful voice, that their future lay not in humdrum everyday employment, but in the exciting limelight of vaudeville. Gordon was easily swayed by his ever-persuasive boss, actually believing that their comedy-with-music act could take the country by storm.

At first, they began to steal an hour or two off from their workdays in order to rehearse the act. But gradually the affairs of Shapiro, Bernstein & Co. became so neglected that an executive was sent from the home office to investigate. When asked for an explanation, Chico replied, "I quit." Gordon followed suit, and the two men then hit the road.

After several unsuccessful forays into vaudeville's big time, Marx and Gordon lowered their sights and decided that perhaps it wouldn't be such a bad idea to break into show business at a lower level. So they tried split-weeks and one-night stands. Even then, the team made virtually no impression.

During her favorite son's absence, Minnie was not idle. She turned her attention from entertaining the family to more lucrative endeavors. Changing her name to Minnie Palmer (a more fitting name, she thought, for a theatrical impresario), she moved the Marx clan to Chicago. There, she rented and eventually bought a large brownstone at 4512 Grand

9

Boulevard. The move to Chicago, the boom town of the turn-of-the-century, was logical: The three major vaudeville circuits (the Orpheum, Sullivan and Considine, and the Pantages) used the Windy City as their primary talent pool.

With Minnie behind the curtain as their wheeling and dealing stage mother/manager, Groucho and Gummo hit vaudeville with a fairly popular kid act called The Nightingales. The Nightingales was basically a singing act, and the comedy bits that the boys cooked up were largely inept and unsuccessful. Chico and Gordon were hardly doing better. Arthur sang straight and Chico, between patter in an Italian accent stolen from his barber, accompanied his partner on the piano.

Feeling the act could be improved, Chico decided to bring it to Chicago for Minnie's shrewd perusal.

"I think you've got something there," said Minnie. She went on to make some suggestions. It took some time to convince Arthur Gordon, but Minnie's know-how was irrefutable. Who ever heard of a tenor who wasn't Italian? From that point on, Chico's partner would be billed as Arthur Gordoni.

This essential change accomplished, Marx and Gordoni once again hit the tank towns of vaudeville. One had an Italian name and performed the very American songs of the day, the other had a German-French name and acted with a heavy Italian dialect. With such a wealth of talent between them, it was a wonder that they didn't make the big time—but they didn't.

Minnie, however, pulled a few strings and managed to book Marx and Gordoni at the Willard Theater in Chicago in July 1911. After being separated from his brothers for nearly five years, Chico had no great urge for a reunion. He was having a ball even if he and Gordon were professionally a bust. Vaudeville life appealed to him; it was as open, spontaneous, and carefree as he was.

But Chico's zest for life had yet to be communicated to anyone other than his friends and family—audiences would have to wait a few years before the brothers finally grouped under the innocuous-sounding name, "The Four Marx

Brothers." In the meantime, the year touring with Arthur helped Chico hone his later trademark: his "tootsie-fruitsie ice-a-cream" banter.

Ethnic characterizations were staples of show business. Even Harpo had begun his career (before turning silent) as a Dutch comic. There were no sensitive, highly organized groups in those days to rail against supposed insults. But if there had been, Chico would have had greater success charming them one at a time out of their resentments than he was currently having performing before large audiences. Any Italian coming backstage to ask if he were really a fellow countryman would get an enormous grin, a hug, and a kiss, as Chico would warmly exclaim, *"Paisan!"* Any Jew coming backstage would find Chico equally agreeable to admitting he was a Jew.

There was a basic sameness, however, to the two "Italians," Marx and Gordoni, and the other vaudevillians performing in the same dialect. Even audiences in the most bucolic reaches of Iowa had heard the same routines time and again:

"Where do you work-a, John?"

"On the Delaware-Lackawan."

"And what do you do-a, John?"

"Ah poosh, ah poosh, ah poosh."

Inevitably, as far as Chico and dunning gamblers were concerned, "poosh" came to shove. The team wasn't making any great amount of money, yet Chico consistently managed to lose his share, as well as Gordon's. His younger partner was as big a patsy for Chico as Chico himself proved to be for organized gamblers later in his life.

Since he was older and had a business background, Chico automatically had become the manager of the act, making all the deals, collecting all the money, and "paying" Arthur Gordon.

Years later, Arthur told me that in all the time the two men were partners, he never saw a salary. Chico fed him, roomed with him, paid for his laundry, and gave him fifty cents a week for a haircut.

11

Arthur received dozens of believable excuses for their lack of cash. But it wasn't until later that he found out both their salaries were being gambled away.

On one occasion, after Chico had lost every penny they had, he was warned by the sheriff to pay his bill at the boardinghouse where they were staying. If he didn't, he was told, he'd better get out of town that same night, and the team's luggage would be kept as security. Of course, Chico had not only cashed in but had already lost the money for their railroad tickets.

Somewhere in his travels, Chico had observed a foolproof plan for picking up some quick money. Now was the time to put it in action.

"Whenever you see me go in a place," Chico told Arthur, "give me a few minutes and then follow me inside. But pretend you don't know me."

Arthur knew Chico well enough to have some serious doubts about the enterprise. Chico was his usual reassuring self, however, and Arthur reluctantly went along with the plan.

In the meantime, Chico got the boardinghouse manager to agree that Gordon was a boarder if anyone should ask him.

The plan set up, Chico entered a dry goods store and struck up a conversation with the clerk and some of the customers. The talk turned to that afternoon's ball game. Chico astonished everyone by saying he had a strong hunch and, betting on the underdog, offered ten-to-one odds on the outcome. He could barely keep track of the takers.

He then looked around the store, ostensibly to find a disinterested party to hold the bets. In the meantime, Arthur had quietly entered the store during the heat of the discussion and stood in a corner, innocently examining some shirts.

"He looks like an honest man," Chico told the others. "Let's see if he will hold the bets."

Arthur, when approached, feigned reluctance to get involved. But he did so at the townspeople's insistence.

Chico whispered to the bettors that they really didn't know much about the man holding the bets. Perhaps they

12

should play it safe. He suggested someone should find out where Arthur lived. While Chico engaged him in conversation, one of the others made a telephone call to verify that Arthur was actually a guest at the rooming house where he claimed to be staying. This fact was confirmed by the landlord.

The bets were then entrusted to Arthur. Through some sleight of hand, Chico gave the impression that he too had placed his money with Arthur. Arrangements were made to meet at the boardinghouse after the game. The winner agreed to take Arthur Gordoni to dinner for his trouble.

After a few minutes of banter, Chico left. Arthur allowed a discreet amount of time to elapse before he too left the dry goods store. The two next proceeded to a saloon where the episode was repeated. Then they moved on to a third store.

After Chico had accumulated enough money, he and Arthur returned to the boardinghouse, took their possessions out of hock, and left for the train station with hours to spare. By the time the winners converged on the boardinghouse, Marx and Gordon were miles away.

Arthur was having enough difficulty learning to be a performer without also playing the offstage role of confidence man. He was receiving a dubious education from Chico, but he stuck it out for a couple of years before the team split up, never having established even a minor toehold in show business. The two remained lifelong friends, however, and Arthur came to our Hollywood house for dinner at least once a week. This would be followed by a card game in which the methodical Arthur would dawdle over his cards with agonizing slowness (Chico nicknamed him Flash Gordoni). After the team dissolved, Arthur had greater success, if somewhat briefly, as Nora Bayes's fourth husband and stage partner.

For a while, Daddy tried a solo act which didn't advance his career any further. He then formed a double act with his cousin Lou Shean, the son of his Aunt Hannah. That act folded after Chico was caught fooling around with one of the girls on the bill, who coincidentally was also frolicking with the house manager. In addition to threatened mayhem, the act was fined and then dismissed. Lou hadn't enjoyed the

13

same fringe benefits with the chorus girl as Chico had. So when Chico insisted the fine was a legitimate business expense which Lou should share, the act folded.

The prodigal son returned to Illinois in early fall 1912, where the other performing Marx Brothers—Groucho, Gummo, and Harpo (a new addition)—were making great waves in vaudeville with their act, "Fun in Hi Skule."

Not one to miss an opportunity for a laugh, Chico decided to surprise his brothers while they were playing one night in Waukegan, Illinois. The act opened with Harpo walking on stage to where Groucho sat behind a school desk. Harpo's hat had fruit stuck all over it so that it resembled a Hawaiian dessert. Right away Harpo noticed that something was wrong. Groucho was staring unblinkingly at a spot in the orchestra pit. As he turned to follow his brother's gaze, Harpo heard some familiar piano playing. Then he saw what had bewitched Groucho into silence: Chico was insolently plinking the piano keys. Harpo did the first thing that came naturally, tore an apple off his hat and sent it flying at Chico. Chico caught it and threw it at Groucho, who threw it at Gummo, who, hearing the commotion on stage, had stuck his head out of the wing to see what was going on. The show stopped on a fruit-splattered stage. The audience, unaware that it had just watched a brotherly reunion Marx-style, yelled and clapped for more.

Chico was never again to leave his show business brotherhood. His return to the fold provided the necessary catalyst to get the Marxes rolling in a big way.

A good part of their ensuing fame and fortune can be attributed to my father in another respect: Chico gradually took over the management of the act. He realized very early that Minnie, while an enthusiastic amateur, lacked the expertise to become a big league manager. It certainly was true too that Minnie's winsome ways lacked subtlety. She often used

14

samples of Frenchy's cooking to get on the good side of booking agents, and she routinely sent bookers piece goods from Frenchy's tailor shop.

Chico argued that the act was too good for such selling techniques and persuaded the reluctant Minnie into retiring to the family home in Chicago and acting like a full-time mother for a change. The fifth brother, Zeppo, while still a pre-teen, was being very difficult—following in the footsteps of his eldest brother.

Chico saved his mother's feelings by consulting her on every move, listening intently, and then proceeding to do what he thought best. By paying Minnie lip service, he made her feel a part of everything.

Her favorite son was as farseeing as he was manipulative. He had been exposed to enough third-rate talents to see how talented the Marx Brothers actually were. My father's true contribution to the act has never been fully realized because it hasn't been admitted. In his later years, Groucho would give Chico's efforts some due, but he did it with such a faint voice that no one heard. Yes, he would agree, if it hadn't been for Chico's insistence that they could be stars, they would never have gone anywhere. But Groucho didn't go on to say that they became a better act as a result of Chico's unwavering faith.

The Marx Brothers were simply vaudevillians, albeit talented ones, like hundreds of others when they started in the business. Their artistry would not have blossomed were it not for my father's optimism. Groucho's black and envious moods certainly didn't help them to be great clowns. Nor did Harpo's complaisance, naiveté, and inner security. Chico struck the happy medium, and ran with it all over town, buttonholing any bookers and producers who would pay him notice. He was a wonderful salesman, becoming so enthusiastic that he carried other people along.

"We were just young men trying to make a living," Groucho told his biographer, Hector Arce. Their on-the-road routine was "two-a-day, smoke cigars, play cards, pick up girls."

15

Chico was definitely a lady-killer. His combination of shyness and brashness proved too much to resist for many young girls in assorted casts and choruses. To some degree, his brothers envied Chico's success with the opposite sex, but they knew he would quickly tire of a girl and pass her down the line to their eager arms.

When the brothers had become hits in vaudeville with their act, "Home Again," playing the Palace, part of Chico's past caught up with him in the form of a tall, gawky girl who had worked with Chico in Pittsburgh at Shapiro, Bernstein & Co. as a singer—her name was Sophie Miller. Hearing that Chico was playing in Pittsburgh, Sophie decided to pay him a call, bringing along a schoolmate, fifteen-year-old Betty Karp. Chico was twenty-seven.

Betty was young, vital, and pretty, and Chico flirted and teased her until she agreed to go out with him that evening.

"I knew exactly what kind of guy this Marx character was," Betty later recalled. "He used to do what we call 'three-sheet,' which was to stand in front of full-sized posters of the act with, of course, his picture prominently displayed to advantage. I guess Chico thought it was a good way to advertise himself while picking up girls. When he asked me to go out with him I accepted, but when I got home and thought it over it didn't seem like too good an idea. An actor . . . they're here today, gone tomorrow. If I kept that date with him, I was just letting myself in for a wrestling match."

That night, Chico arrived punctually in front of the theater in a borrowed car, dressed to kill. He waited around for more than an hour, sure that this kid couldn't have stood him up. But she had.

The act moved on. Betty returned to school, absolutely certain that nothing would ever induce her to see Chico Marx again.

When I was growing up, I would beg my mother to repeat, for the umpteenth time, how she and Daddy had gotten married. The details were familiar to me, but like so many children I found it reassuring and satisfying to hear her go through the story again and again. If we were on a train, which was likely enough as I spent much of my early childhood following the act from one theater to the next, I would lean my head back on the upholstered seat and gaze out over the darkened fields and homes and small towns of middle America, listening to her voice.

Now living in Brooklyn, my mother knew a young aspiring actress (they were going to secretarial school together) who had an annoying habit of name-dropping. Betty took it as long as she could and then brought her friend up with the news that she too knew a celebrity: Chico Marx.

The boys were playing in Brooklyn at the time and her friend insisted that she and Betty make the afternoon show. When they arrived at the theater, they caught the act and then went around to the stage door. Betty gave the stage manager a note for Leonard (Chico), and the two girls waited anxiously for him to appear.

Each brother, eyeing the two girls for himself, walked up to them in turn, claiming to be Lenny.

"I couldn't make out who was who with their stage makeup on; and so I just said 'No, you're not' to each of them. Finally Chico came up to me and announced himself. Thinking it was Groucho or Harpo trying to trick me again, I said, 'No, you're not' to him, too. But Chico caught me by the arm and said, 'Hey, you're the little girl who stood me up in Pittsburgh.'"

She was impressed that he had remembered her from their first meeting years ago. She should have been, considering the hundreds of girls he had played around with since then. But Betty was the one that had gotten away.

Chico asked her to come to the theater and then go out to dinner, but this time he didn't show up, leaving Betty to wait under the marquee, hopping mad. Apparently, he had forgotten all about their date, probably being wrapped up in some poker game. "He came over to see me the next day and apologized," she would say to me, smiling. "I couldn't resist him—that was our romance."

Chico was hooked, too. Betty, who was not yet twenty, was ingenuous and totally unsophisticated but full of what Chico loved: verve and spirit. He was twelve years older and had knocked around for half his life. He had rarely encountered any resistance from the girls that he had bedded down, but this one was holding out for marriage and respectability.

Chico didn't have the antipathy toward Jewish women that his brothers Harpo and Groucho showed. Betty was just the type of Jewish girl they shied away from. Bossy and abrasive, she knew exactly what she wanted and wasn't afraid to tell you so. Chico admired her "guts" while his brothers preferred docile *shiksas*. Minnie was manipulative but never openly bossy, and her sons tended to forget that she was Jewish, too. Not that Betty was shrewish (not in the beginning of their marriage, at least), she was just naturally straightforward, whereas the boys were used to Minnie's soft-spoken, devious manner.

There was something else that may have inclined Daddy toward matrimony. Betty was a "good" girl, in the sense

18

that she didn't fool around, and yet she had the kind of beauty that stopped men on the street. She had an exquisite figure, great legs, curly blue-black hair, and lovely olive skin. Chico became infatuated with this girl who radiated sex—and yet who wouldn't even let him get a good-night kiss.

Betty followed Chico to Chicago, and the two decided to get married. They went with a couple of Chico's card-playing cronies to call on a rabbi. One of the men took Betty's arm as if he, and not Chico, were the groom. Betty giggled. "Marriage is a very serious matter," the rabbi sternly admonished before throwing the sacrilegious foursome out of his study.

A few nights later, Betty and Chico were invited to dinner by a young married couple named Rothchild. "Why don't I call a rabbi to marry you two?" the host asked. The couple agreed, and shortly thereafter a rabbi arrived for the ceremony. After they were married, they all sat down to a hearty meal.

Mother later told me she was so naive that she didn't know parents were usually invited to attend. Minnie must have been hurt by this oversight, but she never voiced any resentment. Groucho was so offended that he nursed his grudge and didn't invite Chico and Betty to his wedding three years later.

"You have to have dough to go on a honeymoon, Betty, and we don't," Chico explained to his new bride. So he whisked her off to Minnie's romantic chateau on Grand Boulevard in Chicago. There Betty encountered the Marxes in their native element for the first time.

It seemed as if an army was living under that one roof! Chico and Betty shared a room, the boys were doubled up, and a nephew of Minnie's was there—a German refugee being harbored in the basement, even though the First World War had been over for a while already. Then there was Opie, the boys' grandfather, who had been a circus strongman in his youth,

19

lifting wagons on his back and that sort of thing. Still incredibly vigorous at ninety, he went figure skating in the park. In the evenings, a mob of show business people would descend on the house to eat and make merry. Frenchy had bought a huge kettle—the kind they use in restaurants to boil soup—and there was something bubbling in it all day.

Soon after the newlyweds came home to stay, Chico took Betty aside.

"Listen, Betty," he told her. "The boys and I had a conference about you. I told them that you were just a kid and to take it easy, but they were pretty upset. Baby, I understand you, but that doesn't mean other people will."

My mother was properly chastened. It seemed that her quick tongue and frank manner had ruffled the seemingly unflappable family. For instance, Minnie was always trying to look very young, with her big blonde wig and chiffon dresses. When the family sat down to eat, she would come sweeping down the stairs in a grand entrance. One evening, Betty, giggling as the grande dame of Grand Boulevard took her seat at the head of the table, whispered a bit too loudly that Minnie looked like the Queen of Sheba. Minnie took this harmless joke well, but the brothers became defensive.

"They were a very tight family," Betty said. "I realized that I would be a good wife if I didn't do anything to cause friction between the other members of the household. I had to watch my mouth."

Yet some of Betty's comments were better received. She told Groucho that his recent adoption of a mustache was unbecoming. She couldn't understand why he wanted to cover his beautiful mouth with hair. The criticism took effect, and the next morning Groucho shaved and went back to glueing on a false mustache every night for the show.

But if her husband had laid down the law to Betty, Chico himself changed very little with marriage. His appetite for women hadn't diminished an iota.

"I was very young and dumb," Betty told me recently. "Minnie felt sorry for me, I guess. Some girl would call on the phone for Chico and she would say, 'Don't ever call here

20

again. He's a married man now.' It hadn't occurred to me that he was being unfaithful. If I answered the phone and it was a girl asking for Chico, I would say, 'He'll be back in another hour.'

"It was a long time before I realized what was going on, but after that I was *very* suspicious and *very* jealous."

Betty had no desire to go into show business, but to keep an eye on Chico she went on the road with the show, "Home Again." She had to keep physically close to her husband or lose him. Besides, she was crazy about him and couldn't stand the idea of a long separation.

Exposed to the glamor of moving around the country with established vaudeville headliners, Betty tried her best to get sophisticated fast. She would wear layer upon layer of heavy makeup to give the impression of being a woman in the know, but the effect was more that of a trollop. One night in his dressing room, Chico showed her how to tone down her makeup as well as her speaking voice, and she began her transformation into a stylish, elegant lady.

During the first months of marriage, my mother learned an invaluable lesson as to what made the Marx family tick. Harpo, Groucho, and Gummo each made advances to her. Their code of honor was nonexistent; nothing ventured, nothing gained, they must have figured.

The greater her cries of outrage, the more they went after her: Passing her in a hallway they would casually pinch her bottom, or they would try to get a kiss whenever their older brother wasn't around. Chico's new wife was quite a contrast to the compliant girls they had tangled with previously.

When Betty couldn't take their constant minor assaults anymore, she broke down and told her husband; yet Chico made light of it. The brothers, he reasoned, had always shared their girls before, so it was just a matter of educating the three

21

others as to the whys and wherefores of marriage. The next day, Chico took his brothers aside and explained the situation. "Lay off," he told them. "That's my wife. You don't do that to wives."

Betty began to understand the Marxian morality. She had already seen how Minnie had encouraged her sons to chase after fast women, perhaps because she didn't want the boys to be trapped into marriage. Minnie didn't want to share her boys with another woman, and it must have been quite a shock for her when the least responsible member of her brood had brought home a wife.

Years of touring the hinterlands, seeing the uglier side of people and life, made the boys callous and insensitive. In the world known to the Marx Brothers, only the fittest survived—the daily grind of vaudeville life made them both quick to take offense and quick on the offensive. If Betty couldn't take care of herself, too bad.

My mother was able to travel with the troupe during that first year because her train and hotel fares were paid for with the fifty dollars a week she earned as part of the "scenery" (women who were on stage because they had nice legs). She never had any illusions about her God-given talent when she joined the act, especially not when there were Marx Brothers around to tell her otherwise. In one scene of a musical tabloid number, a boat was pulling out, starting its transatlantic voyage, as the entire company raised its voice in song. When Betty, caught up in the spirit of the thing, raised her voice a bit louder than the others, Groucho whispered in her ear, "Don't sing so loud, Boshke, you're throwing everybody off-key."

In another scene, Betty was supposed to do an impersonation of a well-known dancer, Dorothy Dix, who kicked over a high cane. "I was very excited. It was to be my first time on stage alone," said the would-be hoofer. "I had practiced my part day and night for a week, but I couldn't seem to get my legs to go high enough. So when the time came for me to go on, I kicked over a low cane instead—a very low cane!"

Chico went out front to get a good view of his wife's budding talents. When her debut was over, he walked up to her backstage and surprised her with a warm hug. "Baby," he said, "with your looks, and your legs, if you had any talent you'd be worth a million bucks."

I don't believe that Harpo ever commented on Betty's lack of talent, although he may have realized something extra was needed in the bit that she performed with Groucho. The two of them had a routine "in one"—in front of the curtain, behind which the scenery was being changed—in which Betty would walk off the stage snapping her fingers. Then Harpo would come on. One day Harpo must have thought it would be funny if he stuck his foot between Betty's legs as she passed. Betty fell in a graceless leap while the audience howled. Anything for a laugh.

But the spontaneity of the show was an intrinsic part of its popularity—no script would ever hold the team to its appointed lines for long. Anyone who had seen them on stage in vaudeville, and later on Broadway, would realize that their film work, although it preserved their performances for future Marx lovers, could never capture the zany quality of their live work.

Taking "Home Again" on the road was an incredibly taxing process, involving train scheduling, hotel booking, and moving wardrobe and scenery from one state to the next—not to mention having to put up with the various "amenities" of theater owners, such as this sign hung backstage in four hundred Keith theaters:

Don't say "slob" or "son of a gun" or "hully gee" on this stage unless you want to be cancelled peremptorily. Do not address anyone in the audience in any manner. If you have not the ability to entertain Mr. Keith's audiences without risk of offending them, do the best you can. Lack of talent will be less open to censure than would be an insult to a patron. If you are in doubt as to the character of your act, consult the local manager before you go

23

on stage, for if you are guilty of uttering anything
sacrilegious or even suggestive you will be
immediately closed and will never again be allowed
in a theater where Mr. Keith is in authority.

I wonder how Groucho's leer, or Harpo's goosing of chorus
girls, or Daddy's suggestive dialect punning escaped the
vigilant eyes and ears of hundreds of managers. Perhaps with
a hit, management was able to look the other way.

When Betty became pregnant, she was determined to continue
working in the "Home Again" troupe to keep an eye on Chico.
Her brash manner, though tempered somewhat by Chico's ad-
monition, had not been transformed into the serene, contented
glow that one usually associates with incipient motherhood.
Years later, the family would laugh at my mother's abrupt in-
tervention in a fight that the usually quiet Gummo was having
with a train brakeman. Betty watched as the angry brakeman
started to lift his wrench to silence the caustic Gummo, and
then quickly seized the brakeman's hand and interposed her
large stomach long enough for the other brothers to come to
the rescue. Betty, Chico would lovingly proclaim, wasn't
afraid of anyone. Nevertheless, despite this act of valor in her
seventh month of pregnancy, Chico decided that his sturdy
wife would be better off grounded with Minnie in Illinois
while the troupe continued west.

The Chicago house was closed up and most of the
family was living on a farm in suburban La Grange, Illinois,
which Minnie had bought during the First World War. The
Chicago house itself was always on the verge of being lost.
Minnie had been able to get the house in the first place only by
juggling her books, signing I.O.U.s, and borrowing from the
rest of the clan—at the end of which time she had gathered just
enough to put up $1,000 against the $21,000 asking price. A
fellow by the name of Greenbaum, who also happened to live

next door on Grand Boulevard, owned the lease. Whenever her sons were fooling around on stage, ad-libbing for their own amusement, Minnie would yell out from the wings "Greenbaum! Greenbaum!" and they would know that meant, "Concentrate, or we'll lose the place!" (Years later, Chico would pull himself away from a losing streak when one of Betty's well placed *Greenbaum!'s* cleared his gambling-fogged mind.)

At the time her daughter-in-law arrived on the farm, Minnie was busy in Chicago trying to secure more bookings for the act. Though Chico had officially taken the reins out of her hands, she loved to play the part of theatrical impresario and continued her efforts on behalf of her boys without Chico's knowledge. Unfortunately, sometimes her continuing relationship with the theater did not altogether escape Chico's attention. While playing at the Majestic Theater in San Antonio, Texas, a clipping from *Variety* happened to catch his notice:

> *If this act doesn't increase the average weekly receipts for the season so far, at least the amount of its salary while in your house, you don't have to pay it any salary. Four Marx Brothers and Co. (17 people) in* Home Again, *38 minutes of laughs. Includes references.*

Chico whipped off a letter to his meddlesome mother. "When has any theater manager been honest with actors? We can't work for nothing!"

My father was also a bit angry with Minnie for leaving Betty to her own devices on the farm. Betty was nervous and lonely at La Grange—her only companions being Frenchy, Zeppo, and assorted Schoenbergs. She was put in charge of looking after Zeppo while Minnie was away, even though she was only two years his senior.

Zeppo, apparently fed up by being "bossed" around by Betty, decided to scare her a bit. One morning when they were driving back from a shopping expedition, Zeppo speeded along on an ice-slick road. Betty pleaded with him to stop, sure that they would crash. Miraculously, nothing happened, but when Betty got back to the farm she wrote Chico that Zeppo had almost caused her to lose the baby. Chico was the only one who could control the youngest of the Marx brothers. Zeppo, shaken up by a letter he received from the irate Chico, nevertheless had the *chutzpah* to ask him for any of his old suits. This patched things up between them; Chico admired a hell-raiser anyway—and a brother, after all, was a brother.

When Betty was about to deliver, Minnie told her to come to Chicago and stay with her. Betty moved into the boardinghouse where Minnie was renting a room, and anxiously waited for her ordeal to be over. She spent most of her days looking out of the window, thinking of Chico (and what he was up to behind her back), or playing solitaire.

Betty's mother had married for a third time and was living in Pittsburgh, and yet Betty had neglected to tell her that she was expecting a baby. Although Sarah Karp could not have afforded to come to Chicago to be with her daughter, she probably would have given her the assurance that Minnie so flagrantly failed to do. Having given birth to six children, Minnie had forgotten how terrifying the first childbirth could be, even for the seemingly fearless Betty. It was a long, dismal, racking period—at a time when most women generally receive so much attention, she had to take care of herself.

Her labor pains came in the midst of a howling, night-time blizzard. She withstood them as long as she could, and then heavily made her way down the hall to Minnie's room.

"There's plenty of time," Minnie told her. "Go back to your room."

"I've been having the pains for a couple of hours already," Betty said.

"Then call the doctor," Minnie absently replied, going over the act's bookings for next month. "See what he says."

When she reached the doctor from a pay phone at the end of the hall, Betty was told to get to Michael Reese Hospital as quickly as possible, where he would meet her.

"But how am I supposed to get there?" Outside the snowdrifts were waist-high.

"Call a cab," the doctor said.

"I can't. I just used my last nickel."

"Then stay right there, I'll call the cab for you."

A short time later, the doctor rang up Betty and told her she would have to walk to the corner, because the cab couldn't make its way through the snow to the rooming house.

Betty and Minnie made their tortured way to the corner, the strong winds cutting them to the bone. When they finally reached the waiting cab, Betty was in such agony that she seemed to be frozen upright, unable to sit in the back seat next to Minnie. She virtually stood all the way to the hospital.

In the delivery room, the doctor was routinely washing his hands and moving at, what seemed to Betty, an unbearably slow pace. "Stop washing those damned hands!" she screamed. "I'm dying! Tear me open!"

No one had prepared her for childbirth, and the paralyzing fear made the delivery an excruciating horror. Toward dawn on that freezing January day, a baby girl was born. I was the first Marx grandchild.

Ten days later, we were put on a train to join the troupe, which was playing in Oakland, California. Betty was dreadfully worried that something would accidentally happen to me. Having been told by her doctor that newborn infants have soft skulls, she couldn't get to sleep, fearing that the train's rocking might jar something against my head.

When we reached Oakland, there was no Chico. Minnie had told Mother that she would wire ahead, informing him of our arrival. Panic set in: no husband, no money, and a squalling baby. She made a phone call to the theater where the act was playing, and luckily the box office had Chico's number.

Hearing the anxiety in his wife's voice, Chico rushed like a madman to the depot, putting on his clothes in the cab. After Mother and I were safely in hand, Chico pulled out the laconic telegram he had received a few days earlier from Minnie: "Betty arriving with baby."

Apparently, Chico hadn't taken any notice of me. Mother, back in the hotel room, finally said, "Well, aren't you even going to look at your baby?"

Chico lifted my blanket and took a peek.

"She sure is a funny little thing." Then another look. "She looks like a monkey." What a blow! After all the trouble she had gone through to have me, Chico wasn't the least appreciative. My mother had a lot to contend with.

Shortly thereafter, they heard an angry knock on the door. Daddy opened it. "Get that woman out of here," a house detective said.

"Are you crazy?" Chico protested, all innocence. "This is my wife, and there's my baby in the crib."

The startled detective backed out sheepishly. But Mother knew that Chico had been up to no good—he had probably had a woman sharing his bed during most of the nights that she had spent at La Grange.

The detective's quick entrance and exit also sparked another thought in my mother's mind. Chico was going down to register her and the baby, who was yet without a name. My identity up until then had been pragmatically enough "Baby Marx"—not the kind of name a girl would like to go through life with.

Mother admired actress Maxine Elliot, and so I was named after her on the spot. Most important things in the lives of my family were decided slapdash fashion.

The next day, the boys tossed a coin for the honor of being my godfather, and Gummo won. While the brothers were all congratulating Chico in the next room, my mother overheard him refer to their unexpected visitor of the night before.

"Imagine!" he said. "After all the dames I've taken up to my rooms, the hotel dick finally catches me red-handed with Betty and the kid!" Betty walked out of the hotel room, still hearing their laughter.

In vaudeville, performers closed in one town and rushed like crazy to catch the overnight train to their next playdate. Sometimes it was worth all the hassles, particularly if the show got good notices.

One of the *Variety* reviewers singled out the "Home Again" troupe for attention in his article:*

> *This merry little musical short gives the Four Marx Brothers opportunity to do some very effective work in their several lines. They all have talent, and they shine in this piece which allows them to display their own brand of rollicking humor in which they excel . . . The story concerns Henry Schneider (Julius Marx) who is returning with his family and friends from a voyage across the ocean . . . Milton Marx is seen as Harold Schneider whose chief work is to look handsome, which he does without question. Leonard Marx is seen as an Italian character, and his speciality at the piano, in which he does comic things with his hands and fingers, is one of the best features. He gets a laugh about every minute, is at ease and graceful, and makes good all the time. Arthur Marx is billed as a "nondescript." He is made up as a "boob" and his makeup is not pleasant. He gets a good many laughs but a change should be made in his character. He plays the harp well, and does some comedy with strings that is in a class by itself . . .*

The "Home Again" troupe was full of song and laughter offstage as well as on, and my earlier memories revolve around festive train trips. As a toddler, I loved to fall

*Reprinted by permission, Variety, Inc.

asleep in a hotel room at night and wake up in a Pullman berth the following morning. During my sleep, Daddy would roll me into a blanket and carry me from the hotel to the train. It was all a great adventure, one which came naturally to me, because I wasn't frightened of strange places as most children are.

Trains provided the only constant in my early nomadic life. I never minded being the only kid on a train full of entertainers—I basked in the attention and the shared camaraderie.

Once I obediently crawled on a strange man's lap at my father's urging. "Say hello to Uncle Charlie," Daddy said. The man dangled a watch as he gurgled and cooed at me. That was my earliest memory of Charlie Chaplin, although family folklore filled in his continuing friendship with the brothers. He was a struggling comic at a time when the Marx Brothers were headlining vaudeville tours. They often played in the same cities, though Chaplin's bookings were usually in smaller theaters.

Because they respected each others' talents, they all became fast friends. Once when Chaplin had come to see the brothers' act, he took a newspaper and elaborately opened it, reading throughout the performance, never looking up from the paper. When the Marxes asked if they could see *his* act, Chaplin got them a box. They, in retaliation, sent four Orthodox Jews to the performance, who arrived wearing the traditional Hassidic garb: long black coats, broad black hats, and long, flowing beards. Chaplin outdid himself, but got no reaction from his guests, who he assumed were the brothers in disguise. Finally, Chaplin's pantomime grew so outrageous that the four men in black stood up and silently filed out.

When Mack Sennett offered Chaplin a movie contract, the brothers, impressed by his mastery of pantomime, urged Chaplin to accept it. Only a few years later, Chaplin became the greatest star in silent movies.

Mother told me about going to lunch with Daddy and Chaplin at the College Inn in Chicago. On the street, they walked by a row of garbage cans, and the irrepressible

30

Chaplin suddenly leaped over them and continued walking as if nothing unusual had happened. When they arrived at the restaurant, the three of them were fawned over by the waiters. "There were no waiters at the other tables," Mother recalled. "They were all buzzing around ours. All of them wanted to hear what Chaplin said. I thought at the time that it was a pity he didn't have any privacy. I was glad later that Chico wasn't recognized like that in public."

Life on the road was not all that it was cracked up to be for one member of the act, Betty Marx. Yet there was one distinct advantage to train travel for her: She always knew where Daddy was. He might get caught up in a poker game in the club car, but soon enough he would join us in the sleeping compartment, where Mother occasionally would hang a wet sheet over an open window to create a rudimentary air conditioner for us.

When they were courting, Chico had told Betty how beautiful train travel would be, painting a lovely picture for this child of inner-city slums: broad fields of snow in the moonlight, the pink edges of the peaks of mountains in the Rockies. "Ah," he would sigh, waxing poetic, "Betty, there's nothing like the romance of a train."

When I came along, the romance—if there had been any to begin with—was over. We would arrive in a town, and Betty would unpack at top speed in the hotel before rushing off to the theater for two shows a day. She would have to make time for my breast-feeding, picking me up from the bureau drawer fashioned into a makeshift crib, or from the trunk backstage that all show business children claim to be born in. To top it off, as a baby, I was suffering from malnutrition, and my diet had to be supplemented with various tonics and medications—which meant more running around.

Daddy was *always* happy—probably because he left all the worrying to my mother. He hadn't a care in the world, even if his future for the next ten years was mortgaged to Nick the Greek. Mother felt it was her duty to make the marriage work, so we *had* to tour with Daddy. She was determined, then, to keep me a good baby, so that no one would ever complain about me.

By my second birthday, Mother would boast (more as a sign of her training than anything else) that she could put me down in a room, leave for a couple of hours, and return to find that I hadn't budged.

There was the occasional exception.

It was late on a Saturday night, and I was sitting on the carpeted floor of a strange hotel room, located in Chicago or Detroit or one of those large Midwestern cities where you could get the Sunday papers when you turned in at night. I had never been allowed to stay up so late.

Comics lay scattered everywhere—I had looked at all the color pictures—and I was quite content, watching as my new friends listened to the radio and leafed through the newspaper.

Earlier that evening, in our hotel room across the hallway, I screamed for what seemed hours in the dark. Mommy and Daddy had left me, and a blob of darkness that looked like a bear had been menacing me for an eternity.

"Mommy!" I screamed in that desperation only an abandoned child knows.

"Isn't that Chico and Betty's kid?" a man's voice asked. The door swung open and in walked a couple, silhouetted against the light from the bare bulb hanging in the corridor outside.

Now I was in their hotel room having the time of my life, having forgotten all about the terrors of the shadow bear.

"She's been kidnapped!" My mother's voice seemed hysterical.

The man went to the door and opened it. My parents stood there, Mother in tears and Daddy holding her.

"She's in here," the man told them.

Mother rushed into the room and took me in her arms, enveloping me. Daddy, with a whoop of laughter, turned the scene gay and light. It was all a big game.

32

But when Mother had given vent to her relief, she turned on the couple.

"Why did you take her out of our room?" she raged.

"The child was terrified," the woman replied. "She shouldn't have been left alone like that, all by her lonesome."

"She knew where to find me," my mother cried, stung by the heavy accusation in the other woman's words. In those days, a hotel employee was stationed on every floor by the elevator door. While Mother was in the show, she gave money to the attendant and a bellboy in the lobby to look after me. This Saturday night I suppose they had more fascinating diversions.

"The child was crying her head off," the other woman said, unwilling to back down.

"All she had to do was go to the phone."

"She's just a baby."

"Yes," Mother insisted, "but she knows how to use the phone."

The battle swirled over my head. Eventually, Mother picked me up and stalked out, back to our room, with Daddy trailing behind.

I later found out the couple was a prominent brother-and-sister dance team, Fanchon and Marco, one of the opening acts of the vaudeville program which featured the "Home Again" headliners.

Even at that age, my mother could make me feel extraordinarily guilty. *I* knew she was right. I had only caused her needless trouble.

Soon after this incident, in an unnamed hotel in an unknown city, the Marx Brothers began a series of one-night stands. Rather than bring me along during what was sure to be an incredibly hectic time, Mother decided to leave me at La Grange with Minnie and Frenchy.

As the only grandchild thus far, I was adored by Minnie, and she pampered me and played with me, gladly leaving

33

the more mundane matters of my care to Frenchy. I was her blonde darling, even though my hair was light brown. Mother noticed during her periodic visits that my hair seemed to be getting lighter. Minnie had been putting peroxide in my bath water.

Mother, when she returned with Daddy from the tour, found me terribly spoiled. She didn't have any idea how frightened I had been when she left me behind, and I needed to have Grandma lie down with me until I fell asleep.

To my knowledge, Mother didn't make an issue over this and other matters she found lacking in Minnie's care of me, although I'm sure she had to start my training program all over again at step one. Although Minnie rarely went out of her way to help anyone, Mother was always grateful to her mother-in-law. Whenever Betty and Chico quarreled, Minnie sided with Mother. Betty once asked her why. "My sons love me, no matter what," my grandmother told Mother. "I have to make you love me, too."

I was reunited with my parents just in time to make my first trip to Europe at the age of two and a half. The Marx Brothers were signed up for a London booking.

Actually, the idea of a London engagement had originated with Chico. He was always trying to make the act more successful, and he decided that he could demand a higher salary for the group if they had a European tour under their collective belt. He and Abe Lastfogel, who worked for the William Morris Agency, a group that had recently come to represent the brothers, concocted a six-week London tour. Anxious to get under way before Minnie had a chance to bollix things up, the brothers hurriedly whipped up a batch of old and new material. But my grandmother got wind of the trip and sent them a hurt and angry note. "I am a maker of men," she magisterially penned, "and everything you are, you owe to me." Minnie would not be denied her triumphant entry into London.

We all sailed together in June from New York on the *Mauretania*. The ship arrived in London on time, and so the brothers were able to make their opening date at the London Coliseum, and just as punctually flop. *Variety* accurately reported that, a few minutes into the act, the rowdy audience began to show its displeasure by unleashing a storm of pennies, which shook up the brothers. The hissing started soon afterward.

"We've come a long distance to entertain you," barked Groucho. "The least you could do is throw shillings." That got a laugh.

The show improved somewhat as the brothers began to get the feel of the English musical hall crowd, which didn't understand American slang. Daddy felt confident that he could continue to get good bookings, despite the bad notices. We sailed back home late that July.

Chico's devil-may-care attitude about some things did not extend to the well being of the act. Despite his own self-destructive ways, Daddy was always deliberate and thoughtful about how the act could be furthered. He pushed Groucho from one new venture to the next—which was totally against Groucho's grain. Groucho hated to leave the secure niche which their solid success as vaudevillians guaranteed.

But Chico saw that vaudeville was a dying proposition. Its death blow was struck with the advent of sound in moving pictures. Chico was sure that the brothers had to gamble and make the move to legitimate theater. "Nobody's going to pay three bucks to see us on Broadway when they can see the same thing for fifty cents in vaudeville," Groucho argued. And his pessimism had a certain logic. But eventually Chico managed to sway his younger brother. I don't know how he did it, knowing Groucho's ultraconservative approach to money matters—perhaps Groucho knew deep down that they *were* talented enough to carry a Broadway show.

Chico negotiated a contract quickly, and *I'll Say She Is* opened in Philadelphia in June 1923. Groucho had few misgivings once he discovered that the new show was equally as profitable as vaudeville.

I'll Say She Is was little different than their past acts. It consisted of a number of scenes strung together with hardly any sense of overall plot. But the scenes themselves were great.

The Marx Brothers had honed and perfected their material during the years of touring the country, working forty weeks out of the year.

The show itself may have been sure-fire, but it took a man like Alexander Woollcott to catapult the brothers to stardom. After his rave review of their New York opening (he said he "laughed immodestly throughout the greater part of the first performance"), the Marxes became the darlings of the town. Not that they changed much: Harpo, who was the most successful socially—he became great friends with Woollcott and other members of the literary Round Table—was too much at peace with himself to be changed by being a celebrity; Groucho was too much of a wise guy to resist insulting his admirers; and Chico was too caught up in gambling and fooling around to care much about publicity.

Groucho seemed to be the leader of the group. I knew him as Uncle Gaukee, because I couldn't pronounce Groucho, and I loved him almost as much as Daddy because his love was offered unconditionally, coming as spontaneously as it comes from a child.

I was timid, and Grouch gave me a feeling of tremendous security whenever he held me in his long bony arms. When I would take school friends backstage, he would figuratively embrace them all.

"Are you married?" he would ask a little boy. The kid would nervously giggle, "No," the rest of us laughing with delight.

"Why not?" Groucho would look at him sternly.

"Because I'm five," came the obvious reply.

I wouldn't learn until I was about ten that Groucho could be loving and dear only with children. With adults, he always feared rejection and developed a steel exterior which, with his cruel wit, often made him a sneering, bullying figure.

Daddy used to say that Groucho would insult a king to make a beggar laugh. He would insult the beggar, too, if my experience was any judge. Throughout my childhood, I was hungry for attention and a kind word, but Uncle Grouch's loving ways were abruptly withdrawn when I reached adolescence.

My mother seemed to be the only one who could stand up to Groucho's terrible bantering. She didn't hesitate to tell him when he had spoken too quickly or cruelly. He couldn't stand to apologize, but when he thought it over he would make amends gruffly.

Harpo had been a close second in my affections ever since he had found me backstage one day, scooped me up, and carried me piggyback across the stage. We were a big hit. Any performer can remember that first burst of audience approval, and mine came when I was four.

Daddy loved to tell a story about Harpo during this period. One day as the clan of friends gathered at the Round Table, author and wit Robert C. Benchley was holding forth on the obvious superiority of painting to the other arts. Harpo agreed. "That's very true, Benchley. You know I've picked up painting recently and. . . "

Woollcott interrupted: "Harpo, that's great news! Don't go hiding your light under a bushel—with your great instincts, I can guarantee that you'll be inside the Louvre in ten years if you put your mind to it."

"You think so. . . " Harpo sounded surprised.

"Definitely! Now the first thing we do is fix you up with a show on Madison Avenue—Benchley or I can arrange with someone at the New Yorker to review it—and then you'll be made."

From that moment on, a day wouldn't pass that Woollcott wouldn't badger Harpo for a look at his painting. But Harpo stood his ground. He told him that he was working on a large canvas and that when he was finished Woollcott and the rest could see his work.

But Woollcott wasn't a man to wait indefinitely and one day he and Benchley made a surprise visit to Harpo's apartment. The maid showed them into his new studio. From the doorway the two men found Harpo busily mixing his pallette—while a nude, beautiful young girl stood on a pedestal with a rose in her teeth. Woollcott started to walk over to see the immense canvas that Harpo was working in front of, but Harpo's raised hand made him stop.

"A minute please—I have to add a few finishing touches."

Benchley and Woollcott were amazed. They couldn't get over the fact that Harpo hadn't been kidding them.

"Hold still please!" Harpo called to the nude whose rose had briefly quivered.

"Okay, boys." Harpo motioned his friends over. Benchley and Woollcott bounded over to the canvas. On it Harpo had painted a large banana.

Zeppo and Gummo were never in the running for my love. Uncle Gummo left the act in 1918 and went into the army. He turned to manufacturing women's wear after the end of the First World War, and I hardly ever saw him again, except at family reunions when I would hear his big wheezy laugh. Once, when I was at his house and his son Bobby came home from kindergarten, Gummo asked him, "Well, how'd the first day go?"

"Okay," Bobby said, as his father picked him up for a quick kiss. "Our teacher asked everybody who our fathers were and what they did."

"So did you tell her your dad used to be in show business?"

"Yup. Except I said your name was Harpo."

"But Bobby, you know my name."

"Of course, Daddy." Bobby replied. "But whoever heard of Gummo Marx?"

I didn't know Zeppo at all. He was a big playboy around town, but I found him a cold potato. He was funny, everyone knew that, yet his humor was too much like Groucho's to fit into the act. Groucho never liked that particular comparison—he hated to share the spotlight with anyone. So Zep was left out and had to play the banal romantic leads that we all knew he was much too good for.

It was so easy to gravitate to Uncle Harpo. Although I had seen flashes of his temper, he was usually as innocent and

38

sweet as the world remembers him. I would watch him during intermissions, his flaming red wig on a stand, furiously plucking on a harp he always kept in the corner of his dressing room so his fingers would stay tough (they would bleed if he didn't practice every day). He would have a big Turkish towel wrapped around his head because he perspired a lot under the wig and was always worried that he would get a chill.

Daddy most likely would be doing a crossword puzzle, muttering obscure words to himself. Groucho would be seated in the adjoining dressing room with his copy of *The Nation*, composing obscene letters to the editor, while Zeppo would be on the phone trying to get a date.

The Marx Brothers were all incredibly charismatic characters, offstage as well as on. A few minutes with Harpo left you convinced he was the most wonderful person in the world. The same amount of time spent with Daddy had you convinced that *you* were the most wonderful one. Chico was naturally seductive, even on those rare occasions when seduction wasn't on his mind. Groucho once said that Chico liked the chase better than the kill, and that's probably a fair estimation. He got great pleasure out of winning anyone over.

My earliest memories of Daddy collide happily with each other . . . his lovingly cupped hands over my face . . . running, always trying to keep up with him, finally begging him to slow down . . . "Please, Daddy, I have a pain in my side" . . . his buying me a squirrel coat with matching hat and muff, and the delight he took in hearing me say to another three-year-old how the fur came "from off the belly of a squirrel" . . . running down a snow-covered street in Chicago, trying to catch snowflakes on our tongues . . . his reading the funnies to me every week, each comic strip in a different accent (and me telling Mother, "You don't read as good as Daddy") . . . weaving in and around the posts holding up the Third Avenue el train, Daddy at the wheel, me standing on the seat next to him, hearing him say, "Daddy will bet you that before you can count to five the light will turn green. . . . "

I loved the "business" and got a big kick out of mingling with the cast between the two-a-days. My memories of the backstage life are in broad, garish strokes. . . . I remember the bright lights, lots of them; greasepaint, the most evocative smell in the world; Daddy at his dressing table, darkening his eyebrows, daubing his lip rouge, putting on the black, curly wig to cover his fine brown, thinning hair; and always the excited patter and shouts of the show girls, who were all nude flesh and spangles. It came as quite a shock to discover that my future lay in another direction.

The Chicago house had been sold, and my grandparents had moved to New York to be nearer to the family. When I reached the age of six, Frenchy and Minnie agreed to take me in because I was to begin school in Richmond Hill, Staten Island, that fall, and the show was to be taken on the road again.

I went to the train station to see the troupe off. They would be touring for almost a year, and I longed to be a part of their adventure. Everybody was bustling around, getting seats, putting scenery and luggage in the cars, and a wave of loneliness hit me. I broke down, crying uncontrollably.

Daddy put his arms around me. "We have to be brave, honey," he said, wiping my face. "You'll have to smile at me when we leave. Remember, troupers don't cry."

Very theatrically, I pulled myself together. When the train pulled out, I smiled a slow, melancholy smile. It didn't work. They left without me.

Life at the Richmond Hill home was a far cry from the havoc
of the wild and wooly Chicago days. Some of the old faces
were still there: Al Shean—the Marx Brothers' uncle who was
half of the greatest team in vaudeville, Gallagher and
Shean—stayed there because he was too stingy to buy his own
house, and Tante Hannah, Minnie's sister, often came to see
us. As a devout Christian Scientist, Tante Hannah felt herself
duty-bound to pray aloud whenever the boys dropped by for a
visit. Her mumbled prayers would drone on and on, until one
of the brothers would diplomatically tell her to shut up. Then
she would flounce over to a corner, take me on her lap, and
proceed to give me the same treatment, firmly believing that
as Chico's child I was already a lost soul. (And she may have
had something there.) But Minnie's madcap days were past,
and a stranger would have thought her fairly respectable.

I'm sure that Minnie must have missed the times when
her boys were all under her roof, when she had all her consid-
erable energies bent on making them stars. There had been so
many mouths to feed that she would regularly order half a
cow for dinner. At one point, all five brothers took up the saxo-
phone. This made such a racket that the neighbors called in

the cops to investigate what they thought to be a Marx attempt at duck breeding.

Now that her sons had made it, Minnie was intent on finding other enterprises worthy of her attention. At first she went into the ginger-ale business, but that went nowhere. Then she tried to manage newcomers to show business, undiscovered talents. The brothers had bought Frenchy a car and hired a chauffeur, and this unfortunate fellow, a man whose talents were exhausted after a Sunday morning drive, became one of Minnie's first (and last) protegés. Even I received coaching. Despite what she called my "advanced youth," Minnie thought she could make something of me. So each morning at the breakfast table, Minnie would have me recite German poems phonetically. I had absolutely no idea what I was spouting, but Minnie wasn't daunted by this minor obstacle. When company came, she would have me recite with appropriate gestures, calling out to me at a certain point, "Okay, Maxine, honey, pull out all the stops!" Then I would fall to my knees with my hand over my heart. At that, she would burst into tears.

From early on, Mother had been made the heavy in my family, and being away from her nitpicking and constant rules I felt a great sense of freedom. Minnie was hardly an authoritarian; she was very much like Chico. Each got tremendous enjoyment out of role playing. It didn't matter whether the situation was darkly dramatic or ludicrously comic—both acted to the hilt. Minnie was also as careless about money as her eldest. Uncle Gummo was doing well in the dress business, and she would con him into giving her a few clothes, which she would then hock for poker money.

Frenchy was much steadier than Minnie, and when I particularly missed my parents he would be there to comfort me. He was a dapper, if no longer meticulous, man. Because he was colorblind, he often wore mismatched socks. "Is that so?" he would respond when I pointed it out. His natty attire was usually spotted with food stains.

My grandfather had emigrated from Alsace-Lorraine, and although he always spoke German, his emotional makeup was French. Once when we went to the movies, he embarrassed me by standing up, tears streaming down his sweet face. when he heard the "Marseillaise" played. He was a gentle man who had long ago yielded authority to his dynamic wife. Now he found Betty intimidating as well. Once, after he had taken me to see *The Scarlet Letter*, I asked him why they had put the A on the lady's dress.

"Pshaw," he replied. "Pshaw." After a bit, he added, "Don't tell der Mamma vhat you saw, yah?"

Even though I had great fun with my grandparents, I never really got over the feeling of being abandoned by my mother and father. I deeply missed the sense of being a part of the show, and Staten Island was too much like a sleepy backwater. I began to long for my mercurial father, whose brightness made every day seem special, and I needed my steadfast mother. Without her, I felt rudderless.

Luckily, Minnie's sons were still pretty much their mother's boys, and whenever they had a layover they would descend on their parents with new jokes and stories and empty stomachs. So I got to see my father and mother quite a few times during the year.

One day, Chico surprised me on my way to school in the morning. After he had put me down from a long fierce hug, we walked the rest of the way to the schoolyard.

"Do you think it'll be okay if I go along with you to school today?" he asked, smiling with his eyes.

Before I knew what was happening, he had crouched down at the end of the line of children, who were preparing to enter the building.

The teacher said, "All right, does anybody have to go to the restroom before we go back to class?" Daddy's was one of several hands that shot up. It naturally stuck out further than the others.

"Who's that?" asked my teacher, walking down to where we were giggling. "Why Mister Marx!" she exclaimed. Then she started to laugh.

43

My father got me excused from class that day, and we spent the morning walking together. It was a glorious spring day, and the trees were on the verge of blooming. I felt light and gay, trying to keep from thinking of the fact that we would only be together a short while.

"What is it, honey? I know when you have something on your mind. Tell me and I'll fix it."

I had overheard a conversation between two class-mates.

"You don't really like Maxine, do you?" one asked.

"Not really," came the reply, "but her father *is* Chico Marx."

My father looked at me—I guess he could tell that I had cried about it almost every night since. How could he change the fact that people only saw me as a reflection of him? That overheard remark had crystalized my own unexpressed feeling about my peers. My only claim to being an interesting person was my connection to famous relatives. How could anyone really care about me, a nobody? I didn't realize that to a large extent I provoked that reaction in others by constantly bringing up my family and trading in on their fame.

"Baby," Chico said, suddenly serious, kneeling beside me, "some people in this world just aren't worth caring about. You know your daddy loves you, and that's all that's important."

I nodded my head.

"Maxine, look around you. Spring always makes me feel like starting things fresh. When I start to see the green popping up all over, I get this tingling in my back that makes me want to lift my head up and straighten my back and take a big deep breath."

He took an exaggeratedly deep breath, made his back ramrod straight, and picked up his head. I followed his lead, taking a deep breath, straightening up. Then we marched around the park like tin soldiers on parade. Daddy broke formation by doing a cartwheel on the grass. We lay down in the new grass together, side by side.

"Remember, honey," Chico said, his eyes closed against the bright sunlight, "spring means a brand-new start for a lot of things."

Knowing what I do now, I wonder if my father wasn't talking to himself as much as to me.

The next few years meant a succession of fairly dreary boarding schools for me. For the brothers, *I'll Say She Is* was followed by two other big Broadway hits, *The Coconuts* and *Animal Crackers*. The Marx Brothers were still coming up in the world, and Sam Harris had gotten George S. Kaufman to write *The Coconuts* and Irving Berlin to compose the music for it. Kaufman hated to write for the Marx Brothers because they didn't respect his script—they had much more fun ad libbing. Once when he was backstage listening to the performance of *The Coconuts*, a friend came up to him to say hello.

"Shush!" Kaufman said, silencing his bewildered pal. "I think I just heard one of my lines!"

The Marx Brothers' future was looking very bright, but my parent's marriage seemed as if it would go on the rocks any day. When the boys were playing in Detroit, Daddy snuck offstage, took his weekly paycheck of $500, and disappeared without telling a soul.

"That bastard!" Groucho fumed, after he had been forced to play Chico's part as well as his own for the remaining portion of the show. "Wait till I get my hands on that louse." Groucho couldn't forgive Chico for walking out—it seemed so unprofessional.

His anger turned to worry, though, when Betty told him that Chico had lost all his money at Nick the Greek's in New York and was afraid that the mob was after him. My mother spent a horrendous two weeks, sure that any day she would read how the body of her husband had turned up in some river. The whole show broke down: The chorus girls were crying, and the brothers could only nervously wait for Chico's death to be announced over the wires. With typical Marx insensitivity, neither the brothers nor their wives tried to comfort the stricken Betty. Finally Betty sought out an old girl friend who offered to stay with her nights.

Late one evening shortly afterwards, Chico burst into his wife's hotel room.

He angrily pointed at the sleeping form beside her, "Who's that? What's been going on here behind my back?!"

After satisfying her husband that she wasn't cheating on him, Betty gave in to her shattered emotions and cried. Her girl friend went over to hold her.

"You've got a lot of nerve scaring Betty like this," she said. "You could at least tell her where you've been all this time."

Chico stood in the doorway, looking blank. Then he picked up his suitcase and walked down the hall.

"I'm sleeping with Harpo tonight," Betty heard him say.

My mother never did find out what had happened.

At the train station the following morning, Groucho told Betty that the brothers had bawled the hell out of her son-of-a-bitch husband.

"I'm not going to forgive him for this one," Groucho told her. "He should have said something to me. I knew the bastard needed some dough. Instead of trusting me, he makes everybody think he's wearing a block of cement at the bottom of a lake. I don't know how you can stand him, Betty, I really don't." But in those early years of her marriage, no matter how angry or disappointed she became at Chico, Betty couldn't stay angry with him for long.

My father really thought that he always behaved well to people. Once we were walking along the boardwalk in Atlantic City, and I asked him why girls couldn't be rabbis.

"It's not in the tradition," he said.

"Then it's a lousy tradition."

"I don't know. I'm not very religious. I just try to live by the Golden Rule."

"What's that?"

He explained.

Oddly enough, I know he was sincere, even though in practice the Golden Rule was dropped when it interfered with the Chico Marx rule: If you can get away with it, try; if you can't, try anyway. That evening, for instance, he stayed out all night playing poker. When he returned in the early morning, Mother refused to let him in. I woke up to the sound of their voices, hers on one side of the door, his on the other.

"Come on, Betty! For Christ's sake, open up!"

Eventually she gave in, probably embarrassed by the disturbance he was creating in the hallway. As Chico walked toward her, anticipating a loving embrace, Mother let fly with a jar of cold cream. My father, a trained boxer, through sheer reflex, sent Betty to the floor with an uppercut.

Daddy was immediately contrite. He cradled her in his arms, laughing and cooing over her.

Pretty soon my mother was laughing, too. "Just don't let it get around," she said, rubbing her tender chin, "that your wife has a glass jaw."

I resented Mother's desperate need to stay close to Chico. I didn't realize that he was being unfaithful to her; I simply thought that she wanted him all to herself. Mother often took out her frustrations by lecturing her docile daughter. Chico could always escape from her nagging, but then she had me. I was subjected to a constant volley of tart observations: "You're laughing like a Marx. It's too loud a laugh for a girl" ... "Don't walk bent over like Groucho. Do you want his round shoulders?"

What made her criticism all the worse were her own good looks and innate taste. Every time she took me to

Milgrim's, a chic store on Fifty-seventh Street, I would die of boredom. I would sit on the floor watching her being fitted, knowing I could never measure up to her standards.

But if I was beginning to loathe my mother's nagging, anything I did to make Chico angry totally devastated me.

"Maxine. Did you cross the street by yourself?"

"No, Daddy."

"I don't want to talk to you," he said coldly.

"But, Daddy—"

"I don't want to talk to people who lie," he interrupted. "If you're going to lie like that I won't talk to you. Ever again. You're not my little girl."

I cried and begged and pleaded, but he didn't soften.

Finally, he said, "Maxine, will you ever, ever lie to me again?"

"No, Daddy," I cried. "Never!"

He relented. "I'm glad," he said, taking me into his arms.

Like most compulsive liars, my father worried that I would become one also.

Chico's strong Victorian streak never hampered his own impulsiveness. He could lie, cheat on Mother, lose all his savings, and it would be okay. He always felt that his charm could get him out of trouble. I knew that he was irresponsible, unlike his brothers, and that he was capable of really hurting me, but somehow it didn't matter that much. The moments that we shared together, alone, made up in my child's mind for all the insecurity and anger he made me feel (but which I could never show).

One day, Chico called me over to watch an ant colony lay seige to a dead grasshopper. We looked on for an hour as the ants struggled in slow motion with their feast. This was the side of him that I loved best: his ability to meet me on my own ground without a note of condescension. As we talked about the difficulties of ant life, his eyes shined with the excitement of the moment. He convinced me that this was the most thrilling hour he had ever spent. That was Chico's way and his great attraction. His life consisted of an endless series of intense flashes, and he made the people around him feel it, too. He was a great salesman for the act, because his optimism and drive were so genuine.

A few weeks later, on the spur of the moment, Chico took me to an art museum in Detroit. He had no knowledge of or interest in art as far as I knew, but that day he moved from one picture to the next, wildly in love with paintings for the first time. Standing before a Rubens—a voluptuous nude—he clapped his hands so loudly that a guard turned around. "That's beautiful!" That was also the last time he went to a museum. He had seen what it was like, gotten his fill of it emotionally, and that was enough.

Walking home that day through the park, I eagerly waited for him to start rhapsodizing over the delicacy of the spring day. I had a hard time keeping up with his rapid strides. He suddenly stopped short.

"Honey," he said, "what do you want most in the whole world?"

A red flag went up.

"I don't want anything, Daddy."

"Isn't there anything you'd like to have?"

I realized that I would have to settle for second best. I tried to think of the most outrageously expensive thing he could get me.

"A typewriter," I finally blurted out.

Taking me by the hand, he took me to a store in the neighborhood where he bought me the most expensive typewriter they had. After we got it home, he said, "Now that you've got the typewriter, can I go play bridge?"

I waited for him to leave before I started to cry.

The Marxes were rich by any standards, but Betty was completely in the dark as to how much Chico was making. She scrimped and saved. She wouldn't know how well off they were until five decades later, when she read about it in

Groucho's biography. She called me up, furious about how naive she had been. "That Chico!" she said. "Could you believe I was worried to death about every dollar while my husband was making thousands of dollars a month?" I asked her why she had never asked one of the brothers how much he was making. "That would have made him look bad," she told me.

Gambling had totally enslaved my father. I refused to accept the *tsoris* my mother had to endure. Once, my mother sent me in to fetch him at the New York Bridge and Whist Club. The man at the desk said that my father would be down shortly. An hour later, Betty went up to the desk.

"Tell Mr. Marx that if he isn't down in five minutes, his wife will come up and get him."

The clerk wisely refrained from telling her that only men were allowed upstairs.

Daddy came down, furious. Mother had torn him away from a hot game. He angrily started the car. I don't know what I dreaded most, the loud and tearful arguments or the brooding silences.

"Chico," Mother tentatively offered, "don't forget to make a right turn at the light."

Daddy exploded. "Don't tell me how to drive! I know what I'm doing."

"I'm not telling you anything except to make a right turn here."

"I know where to turn," he shouted. "If you think you know so damn much, you take the car and drive it."

He pulled over sharply, turned off the ignition, got out of the car, making sure to slam the door behind him, and walked away.

Now that we were alone, Mother's temper snapped. "That son of a bitch!" she said, sliding over to take the wheel. "He did that on purpose."

"Where's he going, anyway?" I asked.

"Where do you think? Back to the bridge club."

We went to dinner minus a card shark.

Ironically, if my father was the one brother who couldn't hold on to his salary longer than it took to lose a card game, he was also the successful gambler who made his other brothers wealthy. He charmed and manipulated big-time, hard-boiled producers. Yet, it was all a game to Chico, who believed the act would make it really big; it was just a matter of making the men with money believe that, too.

The William Morris Agency offered *The Coconuts* and the team to Paramount for $75,000. Walter Wanger, the studio's man in New York, took the offer to Adolph Zukor, the multimillionaire head of Paramount. Zukor said no go, way too much money. Wanger set up a meeting between Zukor and Chico.

Chico walked into Zukor's office and solemnly shook his hand. He said, "Mr. Zukor, this is a great moment in my life. You're the greatest showman this country has. Everybody knows what a boost you're giving pictures, how well you treated Mary Pickford. . . . I just have to tell you what a thrill this is to meet a legend."

"So what seems to be the trouble between . . . ."

"Mr. Zukor," Chico began, giving Zukor his most sincere look. "All these years we've worked to make this one show great. The best of our stuff is in it—all the funniest bits. Now my brothers and I want to make a picture for you. We'll give you everything we've got for only $100,000."

"Well, Walter," Zukor said, turning to his assistant, "that doesn't sound unreasonable."

Wanger could only nod his head, amazed at how Chico had walked off with $25,000 more than the original offer Zukor had decided was excessive. Chico had another convert.

So the brothers, like Eddie Cantor and Rudy Vallee, started making their film while still playing on Broadway.

51

They were getting $2,000 a week in their new show, *Animal Crackers*, and now they would be getting double that amount for a couple of months' work. The brothers filmed *The Coconuts*, one of the first screen musicals, four days a week at Paramount's studio in Astoria, Long Island.

Groucho was grateful and proud of Chico—he knew he could never make others believe in the act as well as Chico because he didn't have his radiant optimism. If there was one thing that Groucho did envy his older brother during this period, it was that Chico's optimism carried over to his personal life. Groucho was always worried that one day he would be completely wiped out. A fun day for Groucho meant driving over to his broker's office and looking at his holdings increase. Groucho may have given the impression that he was perpetually thumbing his nose at the established order, but no one yearned for the security of wealth more than he.

Groucho also couldn't understand how a man like George Kaufman, witty and erudite, could have been attracted to Chico instead of to someone more his intellectual equal, someone like Groucho himself. Kaufman immediately liked Chico's warm sense of humor—and, of course, they both loved bridge. In later life, Groucho would tell Howard Teichmann, Kaufman's biographer, how the only Marx Brother Kaufman didn't get along with was Chico. Actually, Groucho couldn't stand the fact that anyone in the literary world could genuinely like his brother.

I was sitting in a restaurant in New York with Daddy and Kaufman soon after Mary Astor's diary came out. In it, she described in vivid detail how good Kaufman was in bed. A man came over to the table where we were all eating and winked slyly at Kaufman, saying, "Just finished reading Mary Astor's book, George." Kaufman turned beet red.

When the man went away, Daddy leaned over and patted Kaufman on the shoulder. "Listen, George," he said, "at least you got good notices." Kaufman brightened up, and they both laughed.

On May 3, 1929, *The Coconuts* premiered in New York and the brothers were, if anything, subdued. Daddy,

Groucho, and Harpo had missed the opening but had caught the film after the Saturday matinee. The audience was not exactly convulsed with laughter.

The boys came over to the house and sat around commiserating with each other.

"That picture will ruin us," said Groucho. "We're going to have to buy it back." The glum trio just stared at each other.

But the reviews were soon in, and the movie was a tremendous hit. It became, in fact, one of the top grossers for Paramount that year, playing throughout the country. Today, when we look at *The Coconuts*, we see its hackneyed plot, its phoney romantic segments, and its clumsy direction, but in 1929 the film was a great sensation. People kept coming back to see it three and four times just to understand the rapid dialogue. The brothers had scored in yet another medium.

In the summer of 1929 we went to Camp Arcady at Lake George, New York. Daddy suggested that we take a boat over to an island in the middle of the lake, where we discovered a beautiful hotel.

"Do you want to stay here for a while?" Chico asked Mother. She said that it seemed like a nice place. so we took the elevator up to look at a suite.

As my mother was looking the accommodations over, the assistant manager, a plump jovial man who tried unsuccessfully to tell Daddy a joke, suddenly looked at Daddy and, obviously embarrassed, asked him if he was Jewish.

"Sure," Daddy answered absentmindedly. "Yeah."

"Then," the man stammered, "I don't know really how to tell you this."

"Tell me what?" Daddy asked, suddenly on guard.

"We don't accept Jewish people at this hotel. Sorry. I'm only the assistant manager."

"Don't worry about it, kid," Daddy replied. "I wouldn't want to stay here."

We returned to Camp Arcady in silence.

I had never thought that being Jewish was undesirable. Chico Marx was a huge star who was cultivated by everyone. I felt mixed up and asked Daddy to explain.

"There are some stupid people who don't like Jews," he explained. "We don't need that hotel."

Later that summer we moved to more congenial surroundings. A colony of Broadway stars and writers had moved out to Great Neck, New York, on Long Island Sound. By this time, Uncle Groucho's family was living there full-time, and we rented a house nearby.

At Great Neck, I discovered how far the Marx Brothers had come up in the world. With the money that was rolling in from the movie and the show, even though he managed to squander a large part of his earnings, Chico was able to indulge my mother in every way. While Betty had decided that she wanted to become a lady, her background had hardly prepared her for such an ambition—she hadn't been taught how to dress or how to decorate her house, for instance. But by closely observing her friends in other prosperous households, Betty was able to act as if she were to the manner born. In this respect, she would have been better suited to someone like Groucho, who was the ideal family man. After the show, Groucho would always rush home to his wife and kids. Mother would have had a heart attack if Chico had done that even once.

But one part of Betty deeply loved Chico's impishness and whimsy. We had a no-nonsense maid named Tillie who was a favorite of Daddy's, and as she passed guests at the dinner table, she would swat them on the back. "How's it going, chief?" she would ask. Daddy would explode with laughter.

With the exception of Harpo, all the Marxes were now married. I had heard it whispered that the reason for Harpo's bachelorhood was that he had planned to marry a certain girl but found out she had had an affair with Chico.

All the wives of the Marx Brothers tried to make the same transition as Mother. Marian, Zeppo's wife, had the easiest time, because she had come from a middle-class family and was a great beauty.

Aunt Ruth, Groucho's wife, remained a woman of little pretention. She couldn't have indulged her social ambitions anyway because of Groucho's basic stinginess.

On a hot August afternoon that summer, Ruth put together an elaborate birthday party for my cousin Arthur. When Aunt Ruth discovered that there wasn't enough silverware for everyone at the table, she fixed her eye on me.

"Maxine, you have to leave," she said, briskly.

"What do you mean, Aunt Ruth?" I asked, not really believing it.

"You have to go home, honey. We have no room for an extra guest."

As I started out the door, Minnie spotted me. She asked me where I was going.

"Aunt Ruth says she doesn't have enough room for me," I said disconsolately.

Minnie, who had a great distaste for Groucho's wife, saw an opportunity to indulge her love of theatrics. She drew herself up to her full five feet and loudly announced, "I'm leaving with you! If there's no room for my grandchild, there's no room for me!"

Off we marched. My grandmother put up a splendid show, strutting angrily, her hand holding mine. When we got out of sight, she slowed down, panting in the heat. Her high blood pressure didn't mix well with righteous indignation. I thought she might have a stroke. Luckily, a cab driver came along and picked us up.

When Groucho heard of this fiasco, he sent Gummo, the family conciliator, after us. Minnie stood in the front door of our house, unwilling to back down. Gummo said that Groucho had embarrassed Ruth in front of all the guests. Minnie said that wasn't particularly unusual—Groucho *always* did that to his wife. Gummo pleaded with his mother to be reasonable. Finally I realized that I had better soothe Minnie, or the day would be a total disaster.

"Grandma," I said. "I don't want to go back."

Minnie saw that I meant it and gave in. She had shown Ruth just how she felt anyway.

I knew that Aunt Ruth's treatment of me was not caused so much by her dislike of me as it was by her envy of Mother. As close as the brothers were, their wives kept a healthy distance from each other. Ruth resented Betty's jewels and furs, because Groucho would begrudge her even a new dress. What Ruth overlooked, though, was the cause of Chico's generosity. He was guilty about fooling around so much and would use expensive presents to buy forgiveness. Also, Mother's luxuries might have to be hocked any day to pay off gambling debts—debts which Groucho never incurred.

Occasionally there were subtle signs between the brothers that rivalry was at work. Uncle Groucho once received a dog from Daddy as a birthday present. My uncle wasted no time in naming the new member of his household "Chico," and took great delight in calling out, "Here, Chico," especially when Daddy was around.

There was less of that kind of stuff between Chico and Harpo, but then those two had always been exceptionally close. Their physical resemblance was so acute that Chico would often commit his adulteries in Harpo's name.

The two brothers had one running bet with each other: Who was taller? For years Harpo refused to believe that Chico was one-sixteenth of an inch taller; he would bet him five dollars, get measured, and lose. One day, Harpo stopped Chico after a show.

"Come on, Chico," Harpo said. "Fifty dollars says I'm taller."

"I don't want to take your money, Harp." But Harpo insisted, and so they both took off their shoes and got a stagehand to measure them. Harpo was more than an inch taller.

"Pay up," Harpo said, smiling smugly. "I finally proved this beyond a shadow of a doubt!"

"Wait a minute. Let's measure again," Chico said. "This time with our socks off." Harpo readily complied, and again he was taller.

"You lose, "Harpo said with his hand out. "Fifty bucks, please."

Chico paid reluctantly. "Come on," he said. "Now that I've paid, what's the gimmick?"

"Gimmick?" Harpo said, puzzled. He padded off barefooted to his dressing room.

Years later, Daddy found out that Harpo had gone to a place that advertised: "Increase Your Height Dramatically." He had been stretched for twelve hours. Harpo's height reverted to normal a few days after he won the bet.

Shortly before the next fall term, I was left with Grandma. Karp and Tillie the maid while my parents spent a weekend at the estate of Adolph Zukor, the founder of Paramount. There was talk that Zukor wanted Daddy and my uncles to move to California. Daddy was being dealt with as the manager of the act. Zukor knew that a good part of Paramount's net profits of $18 million for the year 1930 were from the hugely successful *The Coconuts* and *Animal Crackers.*

Adolph's son Eugene took Betty and Chico up to Zukor's estate in a limousine. They were shown to an ornate suite of rooms where a valet and maid waited to attend them. Besides having his own golf course, Zukor had a private zoo and wild animals roamed the grounds. It was a fascinating place, built to awe guests with the owner's power.

The morning after my parents' departure, a phone call came from Mother. She was in tears. "Daddy died."

I slumped to the floor, hysterical. Tillie took the phone. She hung up and came over to me. "It's not your father," she said. "It's your grandmother."

"But Mommy said—"

"Mommy was upset. It was your Grandma Marx who died."

Minnie and Frenchy had dined with Zeppo and his wife, Marian, and my grandmother had suffered a stroke in the car on the ride back to Great Neck. Frenchy told the driver to return to Zeppo's, where Minnie died that night of a cerebral hemorrhage.

Of course I loved Minnie, but it came as a great relief to hear that my father was fine.

Chico took Minnie's death particularly hard and spent the following days in a heart- and mind-deadening gambling spree. What friends took to be incredible insensitivity, Betty realized was simply Chico's way of escape—it was his only way of dealing with the loss of the mother who was so much like himself.

Coming home from the funeral at Woodlawn Jewish Cemetery on Long Island, Chico stepped into the kitchen where I was deeply engrossed in a book—my escape. He told me how, at the service, Alexander Woollcott had found a gravestone with the name of Tom O'Casey on it. Woollcott leaned over and whispered to the brothers, "There's a spy in this cemetery."

"I better get as good a laugh when I go," Chico said, smiling half-heartedly.

The next two years I attended Ethical Culture School on Central Park West in New York. My family took an apartment on the West Side, and I began to have a "normal" homelife, even though Betty and Chico argued. I ignored the raised voices and slammed doors by immersing myself in books—particularly melodramatic serials. I would intensely follow Elsie Dinsmore through her predictable adventures and cry at all the sentimental parts. It was one way of releasing the tensions that I felt I had to hide from my father. I didn't want to disappoint him. After all, it was great having him home. I got used to the fights about his gambling.

After one particularly bad fight, Chico packed up and walked out. Betty had told him if he didn't stop gambling he would have to go, and he did. All I knew was that when I came to breakfast that morning, Mother was still in her bathrobe and her eyes were red.

"Where's Daddy?" I asked, already fearing the worst.

"Gone," she said, not looking up from her coffee.

I started to cry. "Mommy, what are you going to do?"

"I don't know."

I spent the day in the park, playing melancholy hooky. I thought about how much I loved my father. I knew that his inability to stop gambling was the cause of all the friction, yet I loved him so much that I was happy to blame my mother. If she had treated him better and complained less, he would never have left us. For ten days, Mother and I walked around in a state of subdued shock. We hardly talked.

Then, there he was, waiting for me one afternoon after school. I ran into his arms and buried my face in his strong shoulder.

Daddy laughed. "Did you miss me, honey?"

I couldn't respond. I just clung to him, afraid to let go.

"Would you like me to come home?"

"Oh, yes! Please come home! Please! I'll die if you don't."

"You really want me to come home that much?"

I instinctively felt he wanted me to plead with him to return. "Daddy, I can't live without you. I can't."

"All right," he said. It was settled. "If you want me to come home that badly, then I will. But you must tell Mommy that you begged me to come home."

That certainly was true. Over the next few days, I looked at Mother for some sign that she understood he had come home for my sake and not hers. It wasn't until I was older that I realized my father had simply used me to do exactly what he wanted to do all along: come home without asking forgiveness.

Animal Crackers ended the season in New York, went on hiatus for a few weeks that summer, and then began a national tour. My parents gave up the apartment and sent me to live with Mother's cousin, Flo Mirantz, while I studied at Woodmere Academy.

In the middle of the term, Daddy agreed to come to the school and put on an assembly. I couldn't wait for my schoolmates to fall in love with him. He was sensational, playing a lot of his repertoire and joking with the students. Chico was the only one of the brothers who had a good solo act. Harpo couldn't talk, and Groucho's humor didn't fit into a monologue routine—he always needed to work off somebody. In fact, in the act itself, Daddy was much more of an essential ingredient than most people ever realized. The scenes in the films and onstage are mostly between Chico and Groucho, and Chico and Harpo. Daddy once explained to me that the reason Harpo and Groucho relied so heavily on him was that in any "three scene," Groucho had to channel his remarks through Chico to Harpo, and Chico had to interpret Harpo to Groucho. Rarely, if ever, did Groucho and Harpo have a scene together. The mirror sequence in *Duck Soup* is one such instance of a Harpo-Groucho scene, and there Groucho uncharacteristically does not talk.

Soon afterward, my parents, along with the other brothers and their wives, went back to England for a vaudeville booking. Their pictures had been great successes over there, and they were assured a better reception than the first time.

Daddy came back to America with wonderful stories about the people they had met and the places they had seen. He and the Duke of Manchester had become bridge buddies, and Chico and Betty had been guests at his castle. But, Chico added, those people were kind of boring. I guess the life of cucumber sandwiches and tea hadn't awed the brothers much. "What did you say to the Duke, Daddy?" I asked, thinking of court protocol.

"Hi ya, Dook," he replied in his best New Yorkese.

What my father didn't mention was the deal he had helped close on board ship. The brothers and a group of lawyers from Paramount had assembled in Groucho's stateroom for a new contract. The boys demanded and got twice their salary for *The Coconuts* and *Animal Crackers*. For their third picture, they would receive $200,000—a fortune in those Depression years. The team would also be getting a hefty chunk of the net profits—fifty percent. They had the studio over a barrel—their popularity was at a new high.

Paramount had gotten one concession that was about to change my life. The sound stages at the Long Island facility were not as sophisticated as the newer ones in Hollywood, and so the Marx Brothers had agreed to make the big move to the West Coast. I was told more or less matter-of-factly that we would be going west in the summer.

"Grandma will be coming out with you to spend the summer," Mother told me when she called from California to make the final arrangements for my trip.

"Why?" I asked, my heart sinking rapidly. I didn't want to make the long trip with Grandma Karp. Daddy was genuinely fond of his mother-in-law, as were his brothers, and Mother considered her some sort of saint. But I was ashamed of her ludicrous accent, her dowdy appearance, and her illiteracy.

"I don't want you travelling alone," Mother answered. Ridiculous! I had taken many a train by myself, there was nothing to it. But nothing could sway Mother once her mind was set.

Grandma, I'm sure, didn't love me any less because of my obvious indifference. I had no sympathy for the trials she had gone through—I felt that she should have stayed in the Russian hinterlands where she belonged.

As we were coming into Albuquerque, where on previous trips I had stretched my legs at the station, she asked, "Maxine, you want an ice cream?"

"Sure," I absently replied. She took a dime out of her pocketbook and got off the train.

Grandma was gone for a long time. Our train gave a lurch as it started up, and I realized she hadn't returned.

I looked out the window. Standing on the observation platform of the Super Chief which was going in the opposite direction, the dime in her upraised hand telling me she hadn't found the ice-cream vendor, was Grandma Karp.

I pulled the emergency cord. Our train stopped abruptly. The conductor came running. "My grandma's on the other train!" I yelled. "Get her off!"

Grandma had only the dime with her, and no identification. If pressed, her limited English vocabulary might have been good for one sentence: "Chico Marx is my son-in-law."

Somehow, the company employees got her on the right train.

"Grandma," I lectured her, "you were on the wrong train."

"Yeah?" she asked, unperturbed. "Looks just like."

I wanted to impress on her how serious her mistake was. "What would have happened if the other train pulled out?"

"They find me," she answered, her tone too reasonable and assured.

I gave up—there was no way to impress Grandma with her near-tragedy. Her little eyes looked on everything with the same equanimity. I couldn't wait to tell my mother. "You sent her to take care of *me*, huh?"

That summer of 1930 in Malibu, my life burst forth in glorious Technicolor. I was with Daddy, and he was happily sharing his leisure time with me whenever he wasn't actually on the set filming the Marx Brothers' third movie, *Monkey Business*. The three-bedroom house that my parents rented was in the middle of the Malibu colony, and I was thrilled that we were living back-to-back with Hollywood's elite. All of the houses had servants' quarters, yet none of them was particularly lavish. Each had a square of beach fenced off—in effect, creating big sandboxes—for private use.

Joan Bennett lived next door, and next to her was her sister Connie's house. Both had been divorced and were living alone with their children. Joan would lie on the beach for the better part of each day with Diane, her adorable four-year-old.

"Look at them," Mother would say. "One's a big blonde doll, and next to her is a little blonde doll." Despite the pretty picture, I nevertheless thought Diane looked lost and lonely.

Mother was analytical about the Bennett sisters. "Joan is prettier and friendlier," she said, but Connie's a woman like Dietrich. She isn't so beautiful, she's a rail. But the moment you meet her, you know she's somebody."

John Gilbert, the Clark Gable of silent movies, had a house on the other side of ours. Future movie historians would inform me that these weren't his happiest times. They didn't have to.

Our Schnauzer, Curt, was partly responsible for Gilbert's current discomfort. Curt snarled and barked at the waves of the Pacific, and the previous summer, while we were staying at the Croydon Hotel in Manhattan, he had reacted the same way to a cake of ice that was being delivered to the hotel kitchen. He had some kind of neurotic aversion to water, but he was really gentle underneath. All you had to do was say "Shut up, Curt!" and he would stop barking.

One day, Curt got out of our fenced-in yard and began barking ferociously at the waves. Gilbert, who was in the water at the time, thought the dog was barking at him, and wouldn't come out. I ran down to the beach and grabbed Curt. "Come on out, Mr. Gilbert." I called to him. "He won't hurt you."

It must have been humiliating for a man of his fearless and dashing image to have a young girl save him from an overgrown puppy. "You ought to lock up that goddamned dog," Gilbert said, scowling. "He's a menace."

A few days later, while Gilbert was sitting on the beach with a girl, Curt used his back as a fire plug. When the actor came to our house that night, Daddy was apologetic. "Nonsense," Gilbert said. "Even the dogs know where I'm going."

He had been drinking at the time, but it was true. Talking pictures had virtually ended his career as a romantic lead. I had heard it said that the technicians didn't like him and had done something to the sound in his pictures. The great lover came across in a squeaky falsetto.

Garbo, who had had a big affair with him, insisted that Gilbert play the lead in *Queen Christina* in a vain attempt to save his career. During the evening at our house, he railed against Louis B. Mayer, whom he blamed for thwarting his marriage to Garbo. "We were going to run off and Mayer found out," he told Daddy. "He scotched it. The bastard ruined my life." I went to bed before Gilbert passed out. The next morning Daddy expressed sympathy for the actor.

Since my arrival in Malibu, I had made friends with another neighbor, Elaine, the daughter of Adela Roberts St. John, the famous Hearst writer.

Elaine and I stood with our chins over the fence the night Joan Bennett gave a party. Tables and chairs were set up outside her house. Both of us were star-struck and watched in silent awe as movie people wined and dined. During the evening, a familiar figure waved to us. I had my autograph book ready.

Walter Huston came over to us and teased us for being up past our bedtime. After he gave me his autograph, he pointed out a man standing beside a group of laughing people.

"That guy over there's somebody you oughta get. He's going to be a much bigger star than I am."

"Who's that?"

"Spencer Tracy."

I had never heard of him.

When I met Mitzi Green, the child star at Paramount, I asked Mother if she could spend the weekend as my guest in Malibu. Mitzi explained that she wanted to add Daddy to her list of people she could imitate. She was an aspiring mimic, and how she could change the shape of her cute round face into George Arliss's long saturnine one was beyond me.

Mrs. Green was the original stage mother, obsessed with the notion that her daughter would be a great star one day. Once Mrs. Green met Mother, Mitzi was allowed to come over—I guess we passed muster.

After dinner, Daddy and Mitzi sat down at the piano the first night she visited. He went through some of his routines while she intently studied his expression and movements, and then she asked him to do his accent. When he finished, Mitzi threw up her hands in frustration. "There's nothing I can grab a hold of!"

Mitzi was a strange mixture, wise to the ways of show business but as sheltered as I by her overprotective mother. She had started in pictures at the age of six and had quickly achieved feature billing.

I admired her enormous discipline. As we prepared for bed, she took out some cream and spread it over her face.

"What are you doing?" I asked.

"It's a freckle remover."

"Does it work?"

"It hasn't yet," she replied, rubbing it in diligently, "but I keep hoping."

During the course of the summer, Uncle Groucho, who was never shy about requesting things if it could save him money, called Daddy and asked if he could come out and spend some time on the beach. Chico agreed and as soon as Groucho and his family arrived, Mother and Daddy went on a short vacation.

Before they left, Mother took me aside. "Remember that Uncle Groucho and Ruth are our guests," she told me. "You're in charge, and I want you to make sure that they have everything they need."

We had a wonderful time. I adored both my cousins, Arthur and Miriam, and I established a close rapport with Groucho and Ruth. I was relaxed as I could be around my uncle—I had never entirely shaken my fear of his caustic wit—and was eager to please.

His good-natured teasing was delicious. He would call me from all parts of the house. "Here I am, Uncle Groucho," I would say.

"I know you are," he would answer, "because you just said you were."

This exchange was repeated dozens of times, leaving me bewildered and happy. When it palled, he switched to another routine.

"Maxine," he would say thoughtfully, "what do you call those machines they use in war . . the ones with the armor plate and guns?"

"Tanks."

"You're welcome."

He must have figured out dozens of ways to get me to say "Tanks," just so he could come up with, "You're welcome." Groucho was happy for that week—he had a free house on the beach and servants to watch over his family's needs. But his happiness made me feel somewhat depressed: Chico would never have been in such good spirits simply because he was able to spend some time with Mother and me.

Arthur, Miriam, and I went traipsing all over the area, spying on the great and near-great. There was the red and white cottage where Lilyan Tashman and Edmund Lowe lived. The folklore about her was that she would eat and then put her finger down her throat to regurgitate. This was supposed to have caused the cancer that killed her a couple of years later. The Lowes' house acted as a magnet to the girls who lived nearby. We had heard that every room was decorated in red and white, in the splashy good taste associated with Miss Tashman herself. She was spectacular-looking, my idea of what a film star should look like, yet she had a frenetic core. She never seemed to relax.

One day, I gathered my courage and went over to the Lowes' house. When I arrived, they were standing in their front yard with newlyweds Joan Crawford and Douglas Fairbanks, Jr. Seeing the better-known actress up close was a disappointment. Crawford had freckles, which didn't show on screen, and she was holding a knitting bag and needles. There was nothing worse in my mind than an unglamorous star. I hadn't come to see the stars, however.

"Mrs. Lowe," I said, "I've heard so much about your house. I wonder, could I take a look at it?"

She warmly agreed, and I went in while the two couples stayed outside.

"Who's the little girl?" I heard Fairbanks ask.

"She's Chico Marx's kid," his hostess replied.

"He's bad enough," Fairbanks said, "but the one I can't stand is that Zeppo. He plays for blood, and I think he's crooked besides."

A big "Shhh!" went up when they became aware that I could hear them.

I had no idea what they could be referring to. All I knew was that my father and my uncle had been disparaged. When I went to thank Miss Tashman, I did it with an excessive formality to show that I had overheard what I wasn't supposed to hear. Then, with the dignity of a dowager, I returned home.

When Mother brought up the subject of school, it came as a shock to me. I had forgotten all about having to return East. But the more I thought about it, the better I liked the idea. Though I would miss my parents and the easy pattern of life in California, all my friends in Woodmere Academy would be thrilled to hear about my star-studded adventures. In the meantime, Chico and Betty would be staying in Hollywood to do *Horsefeathers*.

So that fall I returned to New York, staying again with Uncle Mike and Aunt Flo and their kids. I felt a great sense of family life with them, and school had never seemed more endurable.

In the middle of the school year, I picked up a newspaper and read "Chico Marx Seriously Injured in Auto Crash." I could hardly get through the article. It said that his kneecap was shattered and that he was recuperating in the hospital. After Aunt Flo was able to quiet me down, she placed a call to Mother. Betty told me that the papers had blown it up and that Chico was going to be fine. A very good doctor had been engaged to rebuild his knee. I wanted to leave immediately to be there with him, but she vetoed the idea. Mother assured me that I was better off finishing my term.

No mention had been made about their plans for my summer. I was afraid that I was going to be shipped off somewhere and not be able to see for myself that Daddy was okay. Deep down, I felt sure that something much worse had happened to him and that Mother was covering up.

And then a call came in early May.

"Guess what, baby?" Chico said.

"What?"

"Wait till you see the house we rented. You'll be a real princess!"

"What do you mean?"

"Well, first of all there's a swimming pool . . . "

"Oh Daddy, I don't believe it!"

"And tennis courts."

"I don't believe it!"

"And gigantic rooms . . . and a suite just for you with a pink marble bath."

I hung up the phone and danced around the house. Pools! Tennis courts! I might have been a star's child, but all that luxury was foreign to me. As soon as I heard my father's description of our new life, I knew what I wanted. I wanted that house; I wanted the glitter and glamor of Hollywood. It didn't matter to me then that I would only be known as Chico's little girl.

Until he was able to continue filming, Chico's accident had postponed *Horsefeathers* for ten weeks. All of the Marx Brothers' movies had large elements of slapstick and acrobatic humor, and Chico was worried that his knee would give him trouble—especially during a climactic football scene. But the studio was getting restless; they had shot around him for as long as they could and so in mid-June 1931 they resumed filming. If you look carefully, you can see Chico limping throughout the end of the movie.

In early August, when *Horsefeathers* was sneak-previewed, the boys were riding a wave of success. *Monkey Business* had broken box-office records. When the team made the cover of *Time*, Paramount knew that they were real moneymakers. After only three pictures, the boys were the studio's box-office leaders of the year. Although the Marx Brothers wanted to take a year off to do stage appearances, Paramount insisted that they begin a new movie at once.

Paramount couldn't afford to give them a year off. In 1931 the picture division was $6 million in the red. Many of the Paramount players were uneasy. Maurice Chevalier had recently made a deal to do a radio show for $5,000 a week.

Standard Oil of New Jersey, Pennsylvania, and Louisiana wanted Daddy and Groucho to do a weekly broadcast from New York for over $7,000 a week. So before any deal was made with Paramount, Groucho and Chico agreed to go on the air, but they were nervous. Groucho was unsure how his brand of outrageous puns and double-entendres would go over in the puritanical world of radio.

However, Groucho was never one to pass up a few easy bucks, and Chico *always* needed money to gamble. (Harpo got a weekly salary for *not* appearing—radio was obviously not for him.)

The radio series began with Groucho playing an ambulance-chasing lawyer and Chico as his assistant. *Variety* reviewed the team in its "Radio Reports" column of December 6, 1931:

> *Opinion differed on their first broadcast . . . Some say they were great, others thought they were about 50-50, and others couldn't see them at all. Of course, all these opinions come from New Yorkers, so they don't count.*

Actually, the show was fairly well accepted and even renewed for an additional thirteen weeks.

Meanwhile, I arrived in Los Angeles with my girl friend Toby, the daughter of Harry Ruby, the composer for *Animal Crackers.*

At that time, Beverly Hills was a sleepy little town with no traffic lights, separated from West Hollywood by a field of blood-red poinsettias. A bridle path ran down the middle of Sunset Boulevard.

The house we moved into for the summer was everything that Chico had described. Actress Pauline Frederick had once lived there. After we moved on, Uncle Harpo took it for a year and then turned it over to George Burns and Gracie Allen.

Both the house and the grounds were enormous. The property rambled up the side of a hill, where a blue canoe bobbed beneath a bridge that spanned the Olympic-sized swimming pool. The cabana area and the tennis courts were great for outdoor entertaining.

Indoors, on the ground floor, were the living room, dining room, solarium, kitchen, and servants' quarters. The upstairs had separate suites for the three of us.

Chico's character hadn't been changed all that much by Hollywood. Like his brothers, he enjoyed the trappings of success but still wasn't able to resist being himself.

After we had settled in on the first day at our new house, Daddy walked over to his next-door neighbor and introduced himself.

"Hello, there," he said. "I just moved in next door."

The two exchanged solemn handshakes.

"Nice to meet you," Chico said sincerely. "What sort of business are you in?"

"Insurance," came the reply. "And yourself?"

"Smuggling."

"What? What did you say?"

"I'm a smuggler."

His neighbor took a step back.

"Oh, don't worry. I don't handle anything dangerous. Only jewels, art, stuff like that. Of course, sometimes I deal in wetbacks."

"Wetbacks?" The man grew pale.

"You know," Chico said jovially. "Illegal immigrants. Labor. Nice money there. But you have to be careful—the Immigration Service is pretty tough on us."

His neighbor started to pull back again, but Chico clapped a friendly hand on the fellow's shoulder.

"Look," Chico told him, "just to show you I'm a nice guy, if your wife needs a new—almost new—necklace, I'm your man. Or maybe you've got a girl friend . . . "

"Now wait a minute, I have no girl friend!" the man exploded.

"Your wife'll never find out from me."

"I have to go," the man said, beating a hasty retreat.

I grew up feeling that my daddy could get away with murder—and always get a laugh.

When I look back at this period of my life, it is with real nostalgia: Everything was golden. Groucho and his family had moved to be near us, and Arthur and Miriam would arrive almost every day to use the pool (Groucho purposely rented a house with a stagnant pool—"That's one way to keep away company," he would say, smirking). Our family was much closer than it had ever been before. My mother let up on Chico, and he treated her to anything she wanted. The three of us went to football games and the races together, or evenings we saw movies or prizefights. Chico gave my mother beautiful furs and jewelry. He would put a diamond bracelet beside her dinner plate and then pretend surprise when she would find it.

When Mother had to go into the hospital for a serious operation, Daddy made a game out of our visits to her. As we would go up in the elevator, he would call out, "First floor, tonsils and adenoids; second floor, liver and kidneys." The people on the stretchers didn't think it was that funny.

Mother took a critical look at us one day when we were visiting her. This time I was not the one with the slip showing; she zeroed in on Daddy.

"You look disgraceful. Look at how you come to see me. You didn't shave. And look at those pants you're wearing. You're not even wearing a tie. Really, Chico! You come here looking like a bum!"

I was glad Mother was feeling better.

As we were leaving the hospital, Daddy suggested that we visit her the following day. "Be sure to wear your prettiest dress, okay?" he asked. Fine.

The next day, I arrived in my nicest party dress and walked into the hospital room with Chico.

"What in the world . . . " Betty said, looking up from her book.

Daddy was immaculately dressed in a top hat, white tie, and tails. He soft-shoed in and did a little fake tap dance to get her laughing.

I had never seen my mother so much in love with him before.

74

It was some time before Mother was able to act as hostess at dinner. When she did, the first dinner party we had almost had her back in bed again.

During the cocktail hour, Daddy called me over to a white-haired, twinkly-eyed man. "I want you to meet one of the greatest men in show business," Daddy told me. "This is George M. Cohan." I had never met him but had been hearing about him for as long as I could remember. Years later, when I saw Jimmy Cagney in *Yankee Doodle Dandy*, I thought Cagney had really captured Cohan's uncontrived charm.

Dinner was always served promptly at seven, and it was particularly important this time because Daddy and his guests would be going to a big fight. But dinner hour came and went, and there was no sign of food on the table. Mother checked with the new cook. The woman told her haughtily that whenever there were guests at previous places of employment, dinner was held off until ten at night and the cook assumed this to be the case in our household as well. (The practice was so prevalent in Hollywood that Uncle Groucho always ate a full dinner before going out to a dinner party.)

Mother rushed the meal as best she could, and finally to everyone's relief it was served. Unfortunately, it was also half-cooked. We sat down with our guests, Mr. Cohan, Al Jolson, Sid Grauman, and Sam Harris.

Another guest, Joseph Schenck, was unusually frank. He was to be one of the founders of Twentieth Century-Fox and was one of the family's closest friends. "Hey, Betty," he bellowed over my head in the general direction of my mother, "this is a lousy dinner." It was her first dinner as a California hostess, and everything had gone wrong. The men laughed it off, but she couldn't.

She wanted so much to make Daddy proud of her. And he *was* proud of her. Why not? She was everything he wanted in a wife. She was beautiful, athletic, easily adaptable, thrifty, and a good mother.

By now, all the boys admired Betty. Once, when we were at a party with Groucho and Ruth, Ruth leaned over

75

and said in a loud, tipsy voice, "Oh Betty, what a lovely necklace! Did you just get it out of hock?"

"Shut up, Ruth!" Groucho said. "I'd like to see the day that you go out and hock something for me. And just remember, if it weren't for Chico, we'd still be playing some tank town in vaudeville somewhere." That was the only time I ever heard Groucho admit what they all owed to Chico.

We moved to another house before school started. Itinerant life was to be the family pattern over the next few years. We would sublet a place for the school year, then take another one for the summer. But we were gypsies with a difference, taking with us trains of servants, cars, furs, and jewels.

The new house belonged to Lawrence Tibbett. It was on Rexford Drive, north of Sunset, and large and comfortable, though not as spectacular as our first.

Because I had been to private school in the East, I was allowed to enter Beverly Hills High even though I was younger than anyone else in my class. I was also still Daddy's princess, never tiring of hugging and kissing him. Whenever Daddy, Mother, and I went out to dinner, I would scoot into the booth between them. "The two of you are disgusting," Mother would say. "You make me want to throw up!" Daddy would just laugh. "Leave her alone," he would tell her. "She's just a baby." He was so right.

And I didn't mind acting the part in public, either, if it pleased Chico. He probably wasn't at all surprised when I told him that I wanted to be an actress. At least he didn't laugh—which I had expected him to do.

I overheard him speaking to Mervyn LeRoy when the producer/director came over to the house one afternoon.

"The kid wants to be an actress," he said.

"Well," LeRoy replied, "she's got a pretty face. But she has bad ankles, Chico."

"But she has talent," Daddy protested. "Or, at least I think she does." He had been delighted to hear me mimicking my French teacher. I had a good ear for accents.

"Yeah, but with bad ankles, it's hard for a girl to make it in the business."

I knew Mervyn was wrong. I wanted so much to prove him wrong. And yet what he said, and what my father had tacitly acknowledged, would remain in my head for years afterward—robbing me of what Chico had in such abundance: self-confidence.

Betty learned swimming, tennis, golf, badminton, and other sports in order to be a companion to Chico, but Chico wanted to "play with the men." Betty felt that if she could tear him away from his friends (most of whom were also gamblers) he might be able to quit his habit. She also realized that being in Hollywood created other troubles: Chico's infidelities were continuing unabated. She knew that he had the pick of any number of gorgeous women who wanted to have an affair with a star, and under this double threat to her marriage Betty couldn't afford to stop being a private eye. Chico loved to outwit her; it added spice to his amours. All I knew of this struggle was that she nagged him constantly about money.

Mother, like Groucho, was sure that they weren't going to bring down big money indefinitely and that investments were the key to a secure future. Chico never saw beyond the next day's bet. It was the gaming instinct that made him a first-rate manager for the act. But as soon as he finished wheeling and dealing on a contract, the money aspect lost its excitement. All he cared about was pitting himself against the odds, the longer the better: The final result mattered very little.

My mother confided her worries to B. P. Schulberg's wife, Ad. They became as friendly as was possible for two Hollywood women whose husbands were intimates. Ad suggested that Mother remain as close as she could to Chico to offer the competition less opportunity to step in and take her place.

Ad's daughter, Sonya, and I became good friends. We were both shy. She opened up among close friends, but she was miserable when strangers stared at her. She and her brother, Budd, would lie down on the floor of the Rolls Royce whenever they were taken from their Hancock Park house to school. I would have loved to have been stared at in her place.

B. P. Schulberg was magnetic, ugly, but charming. He was rumored to be having an affair with actress Sylvia Sidney. Once, when I brought up going to a Sylvia Sidney movie, Sonya said, "I won't see anything with *that* woman in it!" Her reaction made me feel that we had more in common than shyness. I would recoil involuntarily whenever I saw Chico appraising a good-looking woman. Mother had tried to shield me from his indiscretions, but I had witnessed enough fights to begin to have a glimmer of understanding. It wasn't until years later, however, that I was able to discuss my fears with another person—let alone accuse Daddy of wrongdoing.

Any of my girl friends could have told me that my father was a notorious womanizer. But there was an unwritten rule among us not to bring such things up. All of us avidly read the trade newspapers every morning, and we were quick to identify the participants in the blind items, including the parents of our friends. But we never engaged in such gossip among ourselves: None of us wanted to hear about scandalous adventures involving our own families.

One day in March 1933, I was practicing the piano when it started moving across the floor.

Mother came into the room, shouting, "Earthquake!" Both of us stood still, deliberating about what to do. Finally, Mother suggested we move outside to the lawn, which we did slowly, cautiously, between tremors. Never having seen the devastation a quake could inflict, neither of us was frightened.

This couldn't be said for another Marx. Zeppo had overcome his fear of heights to go to his tailor's fourteenth

78

floor shop to have a suit fitted. When the earthquake hit, he ran down the whole fourteen flights and found himself on the sidewalk with one leg stuck in the half-finished pants and the other pant leg dangling behind.

Zeppo's brothers were in New York at the time for discussions with George S. Kaufman and Morrie Ryskind, who were adapting *Of Thee I Sing* as a film for the team. Zeppo was staying behind to look after their father. A few days earlier, Frenchy, who had come out to California to be with the family after Minnie's death, had suffered his second heart attack in three months. It was so severe that he never rose again from his sick bed.

I often went to visit Frenchy. The end was drawing near, and I would find him babbling. *"Regardez, papa . . . les lapins . . . dans le forêt."* It was the only time I had ever heard him speak French. He was a child again in Alsace-Lorraine.

My grandfather died a few days later at the age of seventy-two. Uncle Zeppo accompanied his body back to New York for burial.

I don't think that Frenchy would have appreciated the flippancy with which his death was announced. The obituaries identified his sons as Leonard, vice-president and secretary of the Happy Home Realty Company; Arthur, treasurer of the Harpo Realty Co., and Julius, president of the Harpo Corporation. The boys didn't mean any disrespect. Death and funerals were something they made light of—especially if the death touched them.

The following month, the Marx Brothers were all back in California for the filming of *Duck Soup*, their fifth picture for Paramount. (*Of Thee I Sing* had fallen through because of a lack of financial backing.) School was out and I was literally underfoot on the set. I spent most of my time rubbing my uncles' and father's feet—they were all crazy about foot massages.

Daddy and Groucho both thought well of their new director, Leo McCarey, though Groucho's enthusiasm for McCarey rested on the solid ground of Groucho's belief that men who could hold their liquor were to be respected (all the brothers were practically teetotalers). Daddy's reason for liking him was a little simpler: McCarey liked to gamble. After losing to Leo for a number of days in a row, Chico decided to fix him. One day before the morning break ended, Daddy walked over to him with a bag of walnuts. "How far do you think you can throw one?" Chico asked the director. "Further than you, I bet," said McCarey, rising to the bait. They bet $50 on it, and Leo wound up and threw the first walnut as hard as he could. It went about a hundred feet. Then Daddy casually sauntered up and threw his walnut twice as far. Chico had filled his walnut with lead.

But if the brothers had been in good spirits when shooting the picture, things looked pretty bleak after *Duck Soup* was released. Both the critics and the public agreed that it was too much of the same old routine. The Marx insanity was growing a bit stale. Ironically, *Duck Soup* is now considered one of the great comedies. Not knowing that their iconoclastic picture would be such a spectacular hit forty years later, the boys were despondent. Reviews like Edwin Schallert's in the *Los Angeles Times* were the norm:

> *Every indication points to the Marx Brothers being through with the movies for the time being. They played the game for what it was worth, but the screen is relentless in its exactions on comedians. It's their duty to be funnier in each succeeding picture, and that isn't anything easy.*

The brothers didn't argue with this kind of assessment. Even Chico, the optimist, was gloomy after *Duck Soup*. "We have to do some serious thinking . . . our asses are on the line," I heard him telling Groucho on the phone. Daddy felt that Hollywood had sapped their spontaneity, and he didn't know if there was a formula that could bring it back.

While plans were made for their next picture, the boys had to find work elsewhere. I woke up one morning to find Chico packed up and saying good-bye to Mother. He gave me a huge hug and kiss and told me that he would be back in a few weeks. He and Groucho were leaving for New York to start their new radio show, "Marx of Time."

Grandmother Karp had never succeeded in becoming truly part of American life. She still spoke Yiddish to Mother, and the English she did know was good for only a limited conversation. Since she couldn't read, I would spend an hour every day reading newspaper articles to her. From her exposure to show business through Daddy and the brothers, Grandma Karp believed that only a very few people warranted coverage in the paper. As she would try to decipher the newsprint, she would ask in her heavy Yiddish accent, "The President?"

"No, Grandma," I would reply.

"Charlie Chaplin?" she would persist.

"No, Grandma."

"The Marx Brothers?"

"No, Grandma."

"Cantor?"

"No, Grandma." The litany completed, I would explain that it was describing a famine in China or some such thing.

When Bruno Hauptmann was being tried in 1935 for kidnapping the Lindbergh baby, she noticed the bold, black headlines. My grandmother went through the usual routine. After it was over, I explained to her what the man was on trial for.

Grandma was terribly upset that anyone would want to hurt a small baby. All of Hollywood, like the rest of the country, was shocked. But in Hollywood, some parents could afford to hire armed guards to watch their kids. "I guess they have to do it because they're in the public eye," Mother said. For some reason, Mother didn't think we were in the public eye enough to worry about such things even though someone had already tried to kidnap me years ago in New York.

Over the next few weeks, Hauptmann's name was constantly in the headlines. Each day I went through the same exchange with my grandmother and would end up telling her what had happened in court.

Then one day there was a huge banner headline: *HAUPTMANN GUILTY.*

"The President?" she asked.

"No, Grandma."

"The Marx Brothers?"

"No, Grandma."

"Charlie Chaplin?"

"No, Grandma."

"Cantor?"

"No, Grandma."

"Hauptmann?"

"Yes, Grandma!!" I could hardly believe what I had heard. "How did you know?"

"That guy," she said, shaking her head in disbelief, "he's still advertising."

82

Paramount was now disenchanted with the Marx Brothers. Despite its long and fruitful association with the team, the studio was reluctant in 1933 to invest more money in a new venture. *Duck Soup*'s rocky start, reasoned the studio chiefs, might mean a lessening of the Marx appeal. There was little the boys could do, except wait until something else came along.

The boys were worried, but in my family nothing had really changed. The Depression had struck everywhere except in Beverly Hills: We had lawn parties, premieres, and backyard tennis games. I had private swimming, dancing, French, tennis, and horseback-riding lessons; and Daddy drove around in a Cadillac and stuffed a huge wad of $100 bills carelessly in his pocket. Poverty wasn't a subject of dinner table conversations.

A vital link in the chemistry of the team had been neglected: the live audience. Working in front of a camera made for a tremendous gulf between performer and audience. In the case of the Marx Brothers, much of the pacing of the act depended on honing it over and over before packed houses. In vaudeville, the brothers were able to do this, developing a sure sense of what worked and what didn't. Their best routines were shaped on the road. But this kind of metamorphosis was not available to them in films. Their first movies were huge successes because they had been hit shows on Broadway to begin with, and their following three pictures had drawn on and virtually depleted their reservoir of "sure stuff" skits from the old vaudeville days. The brothers felt doubly distanced from their audiences: The camera lens cut them off from the people out front as much as their exclusive Beverly Hills addresses did.

Years later, Chico used to tell me how sorry he felt for the generation of comedians who had to grow up in the electronic era. "TV gobbles up their material so quickly that they have no time to develop the way we did. Now there are only verbal comics. All the past greats were more than wits— Laurel and Hardy, W. C. Fields, Red Skelton, and of course, Chaplin, all used acts that were perfected over the years on stage. There's no vaudeville circuit for young guys to go to these days—no growing space."

All I knew of my father's troubles was that he seemed depressed about his chances of persuading Paramount to renew their contract for another feature. He spent his days (when not at the race track or golf course) moping around the house and continuously calling Harpo and Groucho on the phone. Speaking to them gave him a momentary lift.

    Chico: Harpo?

    Harpo: Yeah.

    Chico: What's doing? Did you talk to Goldwyn today?

    Harpo: Yeah. He's only lukewarm.

    Chico: Oh. (Pause) Did you speak to Grouch?

    Harpo: Yep. He's lukewarm, too.

    Chico: Everybody's lukewarm, huh?

    Harpo: No, Zeppo's hot.

(Zeppo had just left the act to become a very successful agent.)

Chico: I called to tell you that I feel lucky today.

Harpo: You say that every day. I'm sick of hanging around waiting for something to break. I'm getting out of this lousy profession.

Chico: Hey, if anybody quits, I'm the oldest and I get to quit first.

Harpo: That's good. You go first and break the ice.

Chico: Ma would have wanted it that way.

Harpo: Right. Well, it's been a pleasure working with you.

Chico: You're swell, too, but a bit noisy.

Harpo: Let me hear from you.

Chico: Keep in touch.

Help came from an unexpected source. One of Daddy's bridge-playing cronies was Irving Thalberg, who thought that, with better management, the Marx Brothers could easily get back on track. Up until then, Thalberg's specialty had been drama. He had huge hits like *Grand Hotel* and *The Barretts of Wimpole Street* to his credit. Now, he told Chico, he wanted to try his hand at comedy.

On a crisp September day, Daddy came rushing home with wonderful news. "Irving doesn't think we're has-beens. He wants to make a deal, giving us our unit—a Marx Brothers unit—with its own writers and directors." Mother and I both hugged him at once. Now the brothers would be working at MGM, where everyone wanted to be.

As Daddy told it, Louis B. Mayer, the head of the studio, hadn't thought them worthy of an MGM contract. But Thalberg had sung their praises so incessantly that Mayer gave in just to shut him up. Daddy had managed, in turn, to finagle an extraordinary concession from the studio: a full fifteen percent of the gross.

85

This was a unique achievement because past percentage deals were usually governed by net profits. Many actors found their percentage was drastically reduced by the time the studio had finished deducting "expenses." That's what happened to the Marx Brothers at Paramount. They might find, for example, that they were paying Mayer's caddie's fees at his golf course. The Marx Brothers would now get their pay straight from the top.

Soon after the team signed a three-picture deal with MGM, Irving Thalberg called them into his office.

"Boys, your movies have a strictly male appeal," he told them. "We have to start giving the women what they want: romance. We need a love interest. I have a new young tenor, Allan Jones, and we'll find a girl to play opposite." (By now, Zeppo had left the act and Allan replaced him as romantic lead.) But a greater problem was the pacing of the films. Without an audience, the Marx Brothers had difficulty timing their lines, and movie audiences often laughed through their best gags.

"Listen, Irving," Chico said, "we've been looking over this script idea you gave us about an opera troupe. It's not for us. It's not funny."

"That can always be fixed. We'll hire a couple of good gag men, and they'll patch things up."

The boys, still smarting under the mixed reception of *Duck Soup*, were not convinced. Groucho was most adamant—he had the most verbal role and was the most vulnerable to bad writing. Chico reassured him by promising to speak to Irving after their customary evening of cards.

The two men, between bridge hands, worked out a solution. Thalberg thought the boys might take several comedy routines on a road tour instead of playing them cold before the camera. They worked out the details that week. The Marx Brothers were scheduled to start at the Orpheum Theatre in Salt Lake City, Utah, on April 13, 1935, and then go on to other vaudeville houses, finally ending up in San Francisco in May. At that point. Sam Wood, the director. would catch their few remaining performances to get a sense of how well the scenes played.

The road tour proved to be the answer. By the end of the tour, the writers had their secretaries sitting through each show, timing the gags. Individual words, lines, and whole jokes were endlessly changed and rearranged during the four daily shows.

The writers weren't always on the right track. They advised that the stateroom scene in *A Night at the Opera*, probably the greatest sequence in the Marx Brothers' most popular film, be deleted. Luckily, Thalberg had the final word. "Leave it in," he told them. "It doesn't work in the theater because the audience won't buy a flat drop that's supposed to be a stateroom. The camera will give the whole thing a more realistic angle—on the screen that room will *look* crowded."

Actually, the Marx Brothers themselves weren't satisfied with the scene. But they didn't wait for the camera to make everything work. All of the brothers had experience "writing" their material although they never put an idea down on paper. They were great ad-libbers. They let their unconscious minds play with the lines, working against one another in a sort of vaudeville one-upmanship. Clifton Fadiman reported how the stateroom scene came out of its cocoon. In the January 1936 issue of *Stage*, he wrote:

> *I went to see Harpo about one thing and another, and he told me that in its original form, the sequence, while comical, was not comical enough. It seemed to go a bit flat. Then one day . . . Chico had an idea. In the first part of the sequence, Groucho is outside giving a breakfast order to the steward. As he finished the order, Chico thought of adding, in stentorian tones, "And two hard-boiled eggs"—and Harpo, not to be outdone, blew his horn. For some reason or other, this gag, properly worked up, of course, made the whole scene jell. It turned something merely funny into something almost pitilessly hilarious.*

The brothers had earned their $7,500 weekly salary.

My father was excited about the new movie scheduled to begin shooting in late spring. George Kaufman, one of the writers for A *Night at the Opera*, had started playing bridge again with Daddy, and then Daddy began to invite him for dinner several times a week. I found myself strongly attracted to Kaufman. He was as sardonic and curt as Uncle Groucho, but as far as I was concerned, much sexier. Mother thought so, too.

Kaufman's style and wit charmed her. It was also obvious to everyone, except Chico, that the writer had a difficult time keeping his eyes off Betty.

One afternoon, Mother's interest in Kaufman underwent a quick reversal. Kaufman had introduced her to his sidekick, Moss Hart, and the two men spent a leisurely lunch out on our patio "entertaining" their hostess. The two collaborators couldn't resist trying to best one another in verbal gymnastics. My mother, never one of the great conversationalists, was made to feel very much the backdrop as these punsters and ad-lib artists preened themselves. "I felt totally humiliated. I wasn't up on these literary gags and inside theater jokes," Betty recalled. "I felt like a boob from the old country, laughing in all the wrong places. Kaufman was just like Groucho: He couldn't resist always being 'on.' " Mother had expected the flirtatious Kaufman to have taken advantage of their time together somewhat differently.

When A *Night at the Opera* was being made, the Metro lot at Culver City became my second home. The Marx Brothers had joined ranks with other superstars, such as Greta Garbo, Clark Gable, Joan Crawford, Spencer Tracy, Myrna Loy, Jeanette MacDonald, William Powell, and Jean Harlow. Stars' children shared many of the privileges of their parents. If I wanted to attend a preview, all I had to do was call the studio. I could eat at the producer's table; I could visit other sets. I was always welcome on the family set because I was well-behaved—meaning I laughed loudly.

I noticed that all the boys found their new director stuffy. Chico particularly disliked Sam Wood, because he never cracked a smile during any of the brothers' routines. Daddy had once heard Wood complain to a friend that he didn't see why the Marx Brothers were such a success given the fact that their humor was totally adolescent, so poor Sam Wood became an especially inviting target for the foursome's collective ill will.

Daddy was the most obvious miscreant when it came to getting under Wood's skin. He perpetually stole five- and ten-dollar bills from the director's wallet. When Wood demanded that the money be returned, Chico sent him a sack filled with pennies.

About two weeks into filming, an elderly messenger with a large white beard rode up to Wood on an equally old bicycle to deliver a telegram. HAVE TAKEN A SHORT HOLIDAY TO HONOLULU, it read. HOPE TO BE BACK IN A MONTH OR SO. It was signed by all three brothers. Wood sagged into his high director's chair, looking pale and breathing heavily. He motioned for an assistant to tip the old Western Union man. The ancient received his quarter and took off his fake beard. "Tanks, boss," Chico said in his Italian dialect, pocketing the change.

Wood was understandably troubled by an upset stomach through most of the picture, and always had a glass of milk delivered to the set with his lunch. One afternoon, the milk came in a baby's bottle. Soon afterwards, Chico led a doctor and a nurse onto the set.

"Okay. Let me see this crazy man you spoke about," the doctor said.

Daddy and Harpo took hold of Wood. "This is a-him," Chico said, looking sympathetically at the astonished Wood. "He's-a think himself a baby again. It's a shame, eh, Doc?"

Wood gathered his fading authority together. "Don't you men have any sense of decorum?" The boys were taken aback by the degree of Wood's anger, and for once they had no retort.

The following day, *A Night at the Opera* was completed. Just as Wood and his assistants were wrapping things up, an old plowhorse dragged a broken-down carriage onto the set. The Marx Brothers emerged from their dressing rooms at a stately pace, wearing white ties and tails. They tipped their high silk hats to Wood and the crew, and Chico and Groucho took their seats in the carriage with a great show of pomp. Harpo leaped on the horse's back and whipped out a small pole on which was tied a carrot. This he dangled in front of the horse as a midget dressed as a coachman cried, "Tallyho!" And they were off.

I rarely saw children of other stars on the lot, perhaps because they felt blasé about seeing the famous men and women of Hollywood, but I was a most star-struck girl. Spencer Tracy was now my particular idol, and I traced his career from the theater to films. I kept hearing that he could be a nasty drunk and also that he was anti-Semitic, but whenever I met him at the studio he was always sweet . . . and sober.

The dressing-room complex looked like a stucco house with separate suites consisting of a living room, a dressing room with dressing table and makeup lights, a sofa to catnap on, and a full bath and wardrobe room. The five suites in Daddy's complex housed Clark Gable, William Powell, Harpo and Daddy, and Spencer Tracy.

I kept waiting for Tracy to notice me. Everyone on the lot called me the "Tracy girl," but he never knew. Though I would lurk about his suite door, hoping, he never came out when I was there. One day I decided to stop dreaming and do something, and so I sat down and wrote him what I thought to be a wonderfully charming and sophisticated note, letting him know of my existence. But just when I was about to slip it under his dressing-room door, I lost my nerve. What if he had shown it to Daddy for a laugh?

One afternoon, Daddy and I were walking to the parking lot when Chico caught sight of Tracy a few yards ahead of us. "Hey, Spencer," he called, waving him over, "my kid here's got a big crush on you." Chico might as well have yelled it over a bullhorn.

Tracy looked down at me with his intense blue eyes and gave me a shy smile. Then he patted me on the head and started to talk to Daddy about horse racing down in Mexico. What kind of "Mike" was he that couldn't recognize my irresistible "Pat"? Of course, I realized as we walked away from Tracy, few romances could have survived such an introduction.

Despite the grandeur of Garbo and the mass appeal of Joan Crawford, Norma Shearer was the grande dame of the studio. Her marriage to Irving Thalberg wasn't exactly a disadvantage. On Thalberg's suggestion, Chico brought Betty over to the Thalberg's beach house so the two women could get acquainted.

Betty was all nerves. She had heard of Shearer's bad temper during filming and was intimidated by her fame. Most of all, she was afraid of disappointing Chico, who was sure that they would get along perfectly.

When Chico and Betty arrived, Thalberg met them at the door. As the men settled down to their perennial bridge game, Thalberg motioned for Betty to go upstairs. "Norma's expecting you," he said. Betty hesitantly walked up the long flight of stairs, wishing she had never come. She knocked on the door. Betty heard a groan, "Oh, come in, don't make me get up." Betty felt like turning around and walking back down the stairs, but against her better judgment she opened the door.

Norma Shearer's face was covered in cold cream and her hair was up in curlers. "Hi, you must be Chico's wife," she said, sitting up in bed. "I'm sorry about this, but I'm really not up to entertaining tonight. Irving never takes my schedule into account—I have to be on the set at 5:30 tomorrow morning."

"Oh, of course, I understand . . ."

"I knew you would. We'll have a little get-together another time."

Mother crept out. Eventually, she and Norma did become good friends. As long as she wasn't making a movie, she could be a charming woman. The two couples saw a great deal of each other, and a dinner at the Thalberg's consisted of a barrage of jokes and juicy gossip.

"Who do you like better, Maxine?" Norma asked me. "Clark Gable or Leslie Howard?" She and Mother had been discussing the merits of various leading men.

I had recently seen Gable on the lot during a break in the filming of *Mutiny on the Bounty*. He was sitting in the sun in his costume, and when he smiled, his strong white teeth flashed against his tan—just gorgeous.

But if Mrs. Thalberg wanted an objective answer, she was asking the wrong girl. "Leslie Howard," I replied without hesitation. He was a passion.

She turned to Mother. "You see, she's got good taste. Anyway, everyone knows that Gable's built like a boy—"

"Leave the room, Maxine." My mother was worse than the Hollywood censor.

There were some things I wished to remain ignorant about, preferring to idolize my "leading men." My friends and I led sheltered and innocent lives. Our Jewish mothers, whose husbands may have been notorious reprobates, saw to that. There was no talk of wild parties, much less the throwing of them. Smoking real cigarettes was considered pretty daring. Most of my friends gravitated to Eddie Cantor's house, where his five daughters operated a big soda fountain and concocted all sorts of gooey sundaes.

Fun consisted of scavenger hunts and moonlit swims, followed by food binges that Henry VIII would have envied. We never smoked pot, took drugs, or stole our parents' Scotch We didn't "let the boys do things."

Yet, we were probably as neurotic a group of young people as could be imagined. As kids growing up in the limelight, we had no need to prove ourselves. We were treated like minor royalty whenever we went out with our parents.

Without them, there was a constant rude awakening: We were nobodies with famous last names.

My first year at Beverly Hills High was a torture. I couldn't see without my glasses, and I was too vain to wear them. I would walk down the long halls, not knowing many of my fellow students and unable to make out the faces of those I did know. One day, a girl asked me who I was saying hello to.

"That guy over there," I told her.

"That's a post, you idiot!"

I remained the most uncoordinated member of an athletic family. Uncle Groucho's children were natural athletes, afraid of nothing. For me, the tennis ball came over the net too fast, and horses had big feet and sharp teeth. I *was* a good swimmer. Mother, who was an excellent golfer, couldn't understand how she had given birth to such a klutz. Her attitude about my lack of athletic skills was shared by the rest of the family. Groucho was surprised to find me doing the rhumba in the living room. "She's a terrific dancer," he cracked. "What happened?"

It didn't help that all the Marxes made friends more easily than I did. Even Mother was out on the golf course every day with Ruby Keeler and Rose Berger, Joe Schenck's niece. Ruby was very quiet—quietly miserable, Mother told me. Her marriage to Al Jolson was pure hell. He denigrated her at ever opportunity. She had no talent, he kept insisting, even after she became an overnight star in a Busby Berkeley musical. He called her family "shanty Irish." Though she had fallen in love with another man, she told Mother that she was trapped as Jolson's wife and victim. "Jolie is really a monster, an ego that walks and talks like a man." Mother tried to straighten her out. "Listen, Ruby," she told her, "if I didn't love Chico, nothing could keep me here. Do what you want to do, and don't consider anybody but yourself." Ruby finally did leave Jolie.

Marjorie, Natalie, Edna, Marilyn, and Janet Cantor proved to be good friends. Dinner at our house was not that conventional—Daddy was always on the phone as he ate—but dinner at their house was disarmingly casual, even to me. At

93

first I was appalled by the way the girls would leave the table whenever they wanted. Two would be present during the soup course, and if they didn't like the salad, they would go upstairs while two others would take their places at the table. Somehow they all managed to be downstairs for dessert.

Mrs. Cantor was almost as compulsive a card player as Daddy. Once, while placing an order for stockings at Saks, she asked for "nines, tens, and jacks."

I wouldn't dare laugh at my mother the way the Cantor girls did at theirs. Mother could really embarrass me. She thought of herself as honest and fair, but often people didn't appreciate her candor. "Look dear," she would say to a friend, "that coat's too long on you; the shoulders make you look like a football player and the color doesn't do you justice."

The Cantor girls shared quarters upstairs, which resembled a girls' dormitory and a not very well-kept beauty parlor. Professional hair dryers on stands cluttered up the room and the girls' chief pastime seemed to be waxing their legs and experimenting with new makeup.

None of the girls were adverse to speaking up. Collectively, they could be as caustic as Uncle Groucho. I could never again enjoy an Alice Faye musical after one of them described her as "the cook's child."

On the other hand, all of them were mad about James Cagney. One evening, as a surprise, Eddie brought the actor home for dinner. Edna opened the door, and before Cagney could say hello she fainted. (I told her fainting was better than getting a pat on the head!)

After dinner, Daddy and I would listen to radio shows together. We loved the same comics, particularly Jack Benny and Fred Allen. Often he would annoy me by finishing their jokes before they did. When I would yell at him, he would grin and tell me, "Well, there are only seven basic jokes."

One evening as Daddy and I were having our usual time together (the hour before dinner that we tried to spend with each other), Chico said, "Did I ever tell you of the time we were in Paris, and Harpo, Groucho, and I decided to go to the races?"

I said, "Nope you never did."

"Well," said Dad, "we started out thinking all we had to do was get a cab and tell him where to go. But you know it doesn't work like that in Paris. We hailed a cab and said, 'Take us to the racetrack please,' and we told him the name '*Longchamp.*' Well, you know the French, all he said was '*Comprend pas*,' and shook his head. Our accent must have been terrible. After a few more tries at saying the track's name as French as we could, he still remained baffled. So then I had a great idea. There was a famous French racehorse by the name of *Epinard*. I told Harpo, 'This will make him understand,' and said '*Epinard*' over and over again until we finally decided that he understood and started off. I felt very smart and told my brothers that they should leave the thinking to me. As we pulled up to a restaurant, the driver said something in French, and I realized that *Epinard* is French for spinach, so he brought us to a place to get some.

"Grouch and Harp said, 'Sure, leave it to you, you'll get us there O.K.' I was damned if I wouldn't make the cabbie understand, so I pulled Harpo out of the cab and told him to get on all fours. I got on top of him and said 'Giddie-up, giddie-up.' and said '*Epinard*' again. Some people started to gather around, the cabbie got a gendarme, and pretty soon it seemed we were going to jail, not to the races, when Grouch yelled, 'Anybody speak English?' And a man came forward and said he did. So we were finally able to explain where we wanted to go. All of them, including the cop, thought it was pretty funny, especially as they suddenly realized what the charade was that we had been acting out. The man who spoke English suddenly said '*Les Frères Marx*' and everyone began applauding—a happy ending."

Another time when Daddy and I were together we heard Eddie Cantor on radio, but I wasn't impressed and told Daddy I didn't think he was so funny.

"Don't say that about a star," he said. "They don't get up there unless they have something special."

I learned how right Chico was when we went to a benefit at which Cantor performed. I was amazed at how terrific he was with an audience.

"Eddie's a great performer," Chico said during the intermission. "He's not really a funny man, but he's a great performer."

Cantor also had the reputation of being quicker to fight injustice than almost anyone else in Hollywood. Once Eddie was on a bill with Bert Williams, the great black vaudeville star, and they stopped off at the same hotel. When Eddie discovered that Williams had to take the freight elevator to his room, Cantor insisted on using the freight car, too.

"That was a nice thing to do," Daddy said when I told him this story. "Bert Williams was a great artist and that wasn't right." My father was oblivious to matters of black and white—in fact, to any sort of social problems. All the Marx Brothers were basically apolitical. When I would get angry at Daddy for not voting, he would say, "What's the use? Harpo and I would both vote on different sides and just cancel each other out."

I loved having lunch with Daddy in the studio commissary. At the producers' and directors' table, a pair of dice was enclosed in a cage-type contraption called "chuck-a-luck," and whoever lost the roll would have to buy lunch for the whole table—just the kind of game Daddy loved. Groucho never played: "Just give me my check," he would rasp. One afternoon, W. C. Fields joined us while he was shooting *David Copperfield*. When he learned that I loved Dickens too, he spent the entire luncheon "hocking me a chinack" about how much this role meant to him. "To play Micawber has been my lifelong dream. I just can't believe my good luck. MGM trusts me with the part." I was surprised to find him so open and enthusiastic, as I had only heard of him as a cynical and taciturn man.

Harpo once told me about going over to Fields' house. "He had a pool table with a cushion on it. He said that when he couldn't get to sleep in bed, he'd come down there and sleep on the table. Then Fields showed me his attic. It was stocked with hundreds of cases of liquor. 'Bill, what's with all the booze?' I asked him. 'Never can be sure Prohibition won't come back, my boy,' he said."

I liked to bring my friends to lunch on the set, especially when I thought we could sit with producer Marcel DeSano. Marcel would always crack us up telling about how many ways he had tried to commit suicide. He told us once how he had taped all the windows of his room, sprayed his favorite perfume all around, put on his favorite record, and turned on the gas. Then he lay down to go to sleep. Hours later, he opened his eyes. If this was heaven, it looked very much like the room he had just left. Only then did he discover that his gas had been turned off because he had neglected to pay the bill. Marcel would tell us story after story, each suicide attempt being aborted in the nick of time through some unforeseen circumstance. The stories didn't seem as funny when a last attempt proved successful.

Oscar Levant, who was close friends with Uncle Harpo, came to dinner once.

"Maxine," Mother ordered, "play for Oscar."

I turned ashen.

"I don't like to listen to children play the piano," he said, saving me from the humiliation.

"Why not, Oscar?" Mother asked. "She plays pretty well."

"I don't," I said, glaring at her.

"I'm not going to hear you play," our guest said, "so forget it."

He wasn't particularly gracious about it, but I was grateful.

Daddy loved to show me off, too. Whenever he introduced me to a Frenchman, he insisted that I speak some

French. I bore it patiently if he spoke to a civilian, (what we called a non-show-business person), but I felt embarrassed if he put me on the spot in front of a celebrity. Naturally, that's exactly what happened when he took me to see Charles Boyer at the studio. "Talk French," Chico said, pushing me forward. The actor spoke to me in French, and I answered him falteringly. He complimented Daddy on my good accent.

"She better have a good accent," Chico said. "It cost me $20,000."

Mother was perpetually embarrassed by some of Grandma Karp's *faux pas*. Grandma meant well, but she didn't quite fit in. There were many such people from the old country in Hollywood at the time, parents of stars and filmmakers who were trying to assimilate themselves in their children's strange world. Because her English was limited, Grandma often had to get by on a one- or two-word response to comments guests made to her.

"Don't always say 'Same here' to everyone, Ma," Betty told her. "Say 'Likewise.'"

Hunt Stromberg, a producer at Metro, visited the house shortly thereafter. As he was leaving, he said, "It was nice to have met you, Mrs. Karp."

Grandma smiled. "Wise guy."

Our family had fallen into a regular routine. It was arranged around Chico's need to be constantly involved in gaming of one kind or another. Tuesday and Friday were fight nights in Los Angeles and Hollywood. Mother and I usually went with him, though Daddy would get annoyed when I would take off my glasses at the bloody parts. Chico was a great fight fan and could call most of the winners, but his biggest thrill came from betting on the underdogs. He wanted the big win against the odds, and, as a consequence, lost his shirt.

Thursdays and Sundays were the cook's nights off, and we would go to the Hillcrest Country Club or to the Clover

Minnie tore Frenchy away from the kitchen to pose for this shot. His tailoring business was not doing too badly, despite the fact that Chico regularly stole the pants from the suits and hocked them for $2.50 a pair—for gambling money. Never the disciplinarian, Frenchy retaliated by making suits with two pairs of pants—one for the customer and one for his son.
(Paramount Photo)

Chico took his new bride to the beach at Atlantic City. Betty, already staying as close as she can to her faithless husband, shows off her legs in the bikini of her day. The brothers are getting to be big names in vaudeville.

Some backstage photographer caught this calm moment in a Chicago dressing room. In the nomadic world of vaudeville headliners, I never felt lost with my parents' arms around me.

Daddy surprised me with this fancy tricycle for my birthday. I didn't have much time to ride it— I had to leave it behind with Grandma Minnie in Chicago when Mother took me with her on the tour of "Home Again."

e three of us popped into a photo studio just off the boardwalk
Atlantic City. Daddy and Mother were on hiatus.
eaters did not have air conditioning, so there were summer
offs for the troupe.

Groucho

A publicity shot, 1925, for
I'll Say She Is, the Marx Brothers'
first Broadway hit! The boys are
dressed for one of the musical
numbers, "We're Four of the
Three Musketeers!"

Surrounded by the entire chorus of *I'll Say She Is*, Chico is in his element. These girls, picked for their legs rather than their voices, were his for the asking. And few weren't asked.

Here are Harpo, Groucho, and Chico looking, they thought, very smart. Chico looks more like a tout than the others. They were obviously pleased with themselves as new stars of Broadway.
(Bill Shipler, Salt Lake City)

Me, Minnie, and Groucho's son, Arthur, in a Manhattan studio. Soon afterwards, Minnie would leave Artie's birthday party to protest Aunt Ruth's treatment of me.

New York City, 1928. *Animal Crackers* was a huge hit and Betty was struggling to keep Chico from losing his shirt at Nick the Greek's. But because he did need money, Chico was willing to go along with Paramount and convinced his brothers to move to Hollywood.

Hollywood, early 1930s. Now the Marx Brothers were certified Hollywood stars and had to take the plunge at Grauman's Chinese Theater. Chico, Harpo, and Groucho clown while Sid Grauman holds Zeppo so we can't see his face. *(Paramount Photo)*

The team hated to pose for publicity stills. On the set of *Monkey Business*, I watched as the poor studio photographer tried to get the three of them to sit still. "Just be natural, fellows," he told them. So they started taking off their pants. When they saw the photographer meant business, they finally smiled for this shot.
(MGM–Photo by Clarence S. Bull)

My dad and uncles enjoying some time at Groucho's house during the late 1930s discussing their upcoming movie *Room Service*. Sitting on the table— Gummo. Clockwise: Groucho, Harpo, Chico, and Zeppo. (RKO Radio Pictures, Inc.)

Harpo and Chico clowning at the Hillcrest Country Club— cheering some publicity agent's heart. They didn't do this too much off the set since people had trouble recognizing them without their makeup. Daddy liked golf because it didn't interfere with more vital matters—a phone at every hole allowed him to call his bookie constantly.

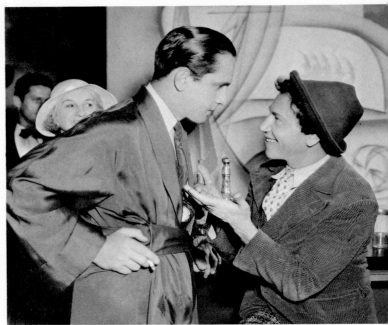

I made a pain of myself getting Daddy to drag stars over to our house for dinner. Here at the Paramount studio, to my delight, Fredric March gets an invitation. *(Paramount Productions, Inc.)*

On the set of *Duck Soup*. Back row: Mom's best friend, Lea Horne, Groucho, Harpo, and Zeppo. Front row: Pop surround by his two adoring women. *(Paramount Productions, Inc.)*

The Thalbergs took Chico and Betty to MGM's costume party celebrating its new movie *Marie Antoinette*. Norma and Betty were just becoming good friends. Left to right: Chico, lady with hat, Martha Raye, Norma Shearer, and actor Brian Ahearne.
(Los Angeles Bureau Wide World Photos)

t my sweet sixteen party. My beautiful mother smiles as Daddy
oks pensive—probably thinking about the bridge game that got
vay. That night all our differences were forgotten.
IcFadden Publications, reprinted by permission of Photoplay Magazine)

This is my favorite picture of myself. I thought I was so glamorous and grown-up. Home after my first year in drama school, I decided I had to have a professional picture for acting work.

Late 1930s. Preview of a picture with Paulette Goddard. Left to right: Mervyn LeRoy, Chaplin, me, Chico, and Paulette. Chaplin shuddered when Chico reminded him that he had held me in his lap when I was two years old.   (*McFadden Publications, reprinted by permission of Photoplay Magazine*)

onald Colman and I (and part of Chico) after the Kellogg
our—a radio show featuring Groucho and Chico as regulars and
nts by Colman, Lawrence Tibbett, Cary Grant, and Carole
ombard. As a professional actress, I was beginning to come out
my shell.

Chico had to continue to work. This early 1950s shot is of his first and only straight part in *The Fifth Season*. Smiling on the outside, few knew Chico was suffering from arteriosclerosis— an illness that would plague him for the next decade.

Shamus and I posed for our wedding picture, 1946. I am finally out from my father's shadow and living my own li[

Chico and my son Brian. Towards the end of his life, Chico only saw his grandsons a few times after Shamus and I moved to the East Coast. "Here, kid," he said to Brian, plopping him down on the piano bench, "let me show you how to shoot the keys."

Club. The latter establishment boasted illegal gambling tables in the back, and Chico would wolf his food down and wander over for some quick action.

One night, when I was about sixteen, he asked me if I would like to play a little. I didn't care for roulette or dice, but I loved blackjack. Daddy introduced me to the dealer and stuffed some money into my hand. "Take good care of her," he told the grim-faced man holding the cards. Then he went off to his own table.

I played for a while and surprised myself by winning much more than I lost. I began to feel the same thrill that Chico must have experienced. People started to gather around me, and I felt like a celebrity.

Suddenly the dealer looked up with a curious smile. "Good-bye, Miss Marx."

I didn't understand.

"Take your winnings and go." The sharp edge to his voice told me he meant it. I found Chico at the roulette wheel.

"The dealer wouldn't let me play anymore."

"How much did you win?"

"Thirty dollars."

"I guess that's all he wanted you to get ahead."

"You mean that he wanted me to win on purpose?"

"He just wanted you to stay away from me. I'm one of their best pigeons. He kept you playing until I was ready to leave."

If Daddy's logic was so sharp, I wondered, how could he keep going to a place that robbed him? But of course Chico was a compulsive gambler. That was the answer to everything.

Daddy's physical energy was enviable. During a hot streak, he would start one evening, play through the following day, and continue on to the next night and day. If he didn't look wide awake, he was still alert. Unshaven, with black circles under his eyes, Chico would make his way home and stumble upstairs to bed. Five hours later, he would be primed for another game. "Winning and losing" had relatively little meaning for him. A great card player, Chico made about $10,000 a year from bridge. But then he would proceed to

99

play reckless poker—a game that penalized those who had to "see" every hand.

Going to the races with Chico was quite an adventure. His pals called him "The Asking Handicapper" because he collected sure tips from the mouths of trainers, owners, jockeys, and I suspect even the horses. There was no way for him to come out ahead betting on horses, but as long as he got to cheer home a winner now and then, his enthusiasm didn't waver.

Unfortunately, Daddy would gamble away not only his own money, but anyone else's cash he could get his hands on. No one around him for long could remain amused by his addiction. When his losses got out of hand, he couldn't control his anxiety.

I could readily identify with the Shirley Temple film, *Little Miss Marker*. I sensed that it wouldn't be beneath Daddy to put me up for security in order to cover a gambling debt. You had to pay your "losses" first—everything else was family and could be attended to later. Chico would sell the furniture out from under us without compunction. Nothing was unhockable. For years, Mother refused to let him buy a house because she was afraid he would sell it without telling her, and we would be out on the street. Harpo and Groucho had come to distrust their brother, too. If he needed money, Chico would get to the box office before his brothers did and collect their salaries. If pressed by large debts, Daddy would also forge their names on checks to raise money. After he had pulled that trick a few times, the brothers got smart and created secret codes known only to themselves and their banks.

One evening, Daddy came home looking flushed and ill at ease. I thought he was sick, but Mother knew better.

"The gamblers are after you," she said unsympathetically. "You owe a lot of money, don't you?"

He denied it. Mother, however, knew her man.

"I just need some rest," Chico told us. "I heard of a resort in the mountains near Denver. Maybe I should go there and get some fresh air into my lungs." He sighed for effect.

Exasperated, Mother agreed to his "holiday," and, yes,

she wouldn't tell a soul where he had gone. By guaranteeing his privacy, she would give him time to make peace with the gamblers. "I'm a nature-lover at heart," he told me.

Under the circumstances, this description of himself was laughable, but there was some truth in it. Chico was fascinated by wild animals and read incessantly about them. One of the high points of his youth had been to meet the man who had brought the first gorilla in captivity to America. When Chico died, he left my sons his collection of animal books.

About his upcoming trip, he said, "I could take long walks, and maybe if I feel up to it I might even go hunting and fishing."

He planned to be gone for ten days. When he returned in two days, he didn't seem particularly rested.

"What happened, Daddy?"

"Well," he said, "when I got there, I looked around and it was even more beautiful than I'd expected. The air was crisp . . . perfect . . . I can't tell you how many deep breaths I took during those first ten or twenty minutes. I felt like a new man. Then I looked around me. There were all these old people, just sitting there . . . doing nothing.

"I happened to have a deck of cards in my pocket. I took them out and riffled them, loudly. Nobody even looked up. So, I sat down at a table and began to play solitaire. Would you believe it? Nobody came to kibitz.

"I don't know how I took it that long. There was absolutely no action! I couldn't stand it. Then, I spotted a little man on the other side of the lobby, looking even more bored than I was. I went up to him and said, 'Pardon me, I'm Chico Marx. I'm an entertainer. What's your name and what do *you* do?' And he said, 'I'm a lepidopterist.'

"I asked him if he knew the name of the rarest moth it would be possible to find in the woods at this time of the year. He mentioned some unpronounceable name. At last I had him. I told him, 'Tell you what. Tomorrow morning we'll go out in the woods. I'll lay you ten to one I find one before you do.' He wasn't interested. I had no choice. I had to come home."

Before signing with Thalberg for a new two-picture contract, Daddy flew to New York to work out a radio deal for the months that would pass between shooting.

"Look, honey," he told Betty, "you can come along if you like, but it's going to be all business and I won't have time to spend with you."

For once, Mother decided to give Chico a little rope. She had played the warden so often that she was getting tired of the role.

"Okay, I'll stay here—Hollywood is heaven compared to New York—but listen, if I hear that you're losing your shirt to those bums at the Whist Club, I'm going to take the first plane there and bring you back. Deal or no deal."

The memory of this conversation passed through Betty's mind as her plane approached Chicago to refuel. It had been nearly twelve weeks since Chico's abrupt departure. She stared at the dark rain clouds through her window, debating whether she was doing the right thing.

The night before, Chico had sounded very peculiar on the phone, as if he had wanted to tell her something very important but couldn't. Was he in some sort of trouble? Betty had decided immediately to see for herself. So now she was on her way to find out what kind of mess her husband had gotten into. Intuition told her it would be best to come unannounced, so she had hurriedly packed and caught the first flight to the East Coast.

The hours on the plane passed pleasantly enough. The man next to her had been extremely nice and they played backgammon for most of the trip.

Betty got off the plane on their brief stopover in Chicago to get a breath of fresh air and some magazines. She had a strange feeling of being watched that she quickly shook off—Chico wasn't around; there was no reason why anyone would be interested in her. In the powder room, the attendant walked over to her as she was fixing her hair.

"Excuse me, lady, but there's a porter outside who wants a word with you." The attendant looked at her meaningfully.

Betty walked outside and found the porter beckoning to her from the shadow of a large potted plant.

"I just thought you'd like to know something," he said in an undertone.

"Well, what is it?" Betty was getting annoyed.

"They're on to you." He seemed to think that was enough.

"You're nuts," she said, and went back to the plane, leaving the porter obviously disappointed at not getting a tip.

By the time Betty arrived in New York, she had forgotten the puzzling incident. Four large men intercepted her at the taxi stand. One of the men showed her a badge.

"Police," he said. "You're coming with us."

"The hell I am," Betty said. "Just who do you think you're talking to?"

"You can stop the phony act, sister," another of the detectives said. "Just get into the car."

"Look, guys," Betty said, getting into the back seat along with two of the men. "You're making a terrible mistake."

104

The first detective turned around to look at her. "You made the mistake by getting involved with him in the first place."

"Who?" Oh God, she thought, what has Chico done now?

"You know who. Dillinger, that's who."

Betty started to giggle with relief.

The detectives were not amused. "Hey, what's so funny? We've got you and now you're going to tell us where your boyfriend's loot is."

"I'm sorry, officers, but I'm Mrs. Chico Marx."

"Do you have any proof?"

"Of course I do. I have something here in my bag."

"Wait a minute," the detective said, snatching her purse from her, "you better let me look at that."

A few minutes passed while the man pawed through her things. "You know you boys can get into trouble for false arrest," Betty told them. Then she started to giggle again as the absurdity of the situation hit her.

"There's no ID here," the detective said, dropping her bag in her lap. When she had changed her handbag, Betty had forgotten to take her wallet.

Nevertheless, she took the news so calmly that the policemen were uneasy. "Is there anybody who can identify you?" Betty thought a moment. "Well, you can drive down to Ruben's and I'm sure somebody there will know me." Reuben's was a famous Broadway restaurant and theatrical hangout.

The detectives decided to play it safe, and they took her over to the restaurant. As soon as she entered, Mr. Reuben rushed over and gave her a big hug. "Betty! Am I glad to see you!"

"You know this woman?"

"Sure. She's Betty Marx, Chico's wife."

The four cops backed out of the door in unison. Betty followed. "Please excuse us if we acted a little hastily, Mrs. Marx," said one of them, "but we had a sure tip. And you fit the description to a tee."

105

"Well, no harm done," Betty said.

"Right." They all nodded their heads.

"You don't have to worry about a lawsuit or anything."

"Thanks, Mrs. Marx," the detective answered. "I just hope your friend feels the same way about it." The four cops started to get back into the police car.

"Who are you talking about?" Betty asked.

"That guy you were playing backgammon with on the plane. We nabbed him too."

Although Dillinger had died a year before, most of the money he had stolen was still missing, and the police were rounding up his old girl friends for leads.

Betty went to the Waldorf without calling Chico. If there is something funny going on, she figured, then Chico won't have a chance to cover up if I surprise him. The man at the desk told her Chico's suite number and she went up and knocked on the door. Chico opened it, cried "Betty!" and gave her a long hug. "What a great surprise, baby! I've been dying to see you."

They had a good laugh over Betty's near-arrest as Dillinger's moll. Then Mother took a good long look at Chico. "Is everything all right with you?"

"What do you mean, honey?" Chico began to look somewhat concerned.

"Do you have any money left?"

"Oh sure, I've got something still   " Chico sounded relieved.

"And have you been behaving yourself?"

"Baby, I haven't looked at a single dame since I've been here. I'm all business." He came over and put his arms around her. "Come on, let's go out and have some fun."

After a few days of shopping and enjoying the night life with a very attentive Chico, Betty went home. She had no desire to stay in New York for long: She loved Hollywood, her beautiful house, her morning golf. When she left, Chico promised her he would be back as soon as he could.

When the door slammed behind Betty, Chico picked up the phone.

"Hello, Ann? She's finally gone."

"Thank God for that! I hate you being married. She's always snooping around. When are you going to get rid of her for good?"

"Annie, we've already talked about that. I love you with all my heart, but unfortunately I'm a married man."

"I've hated staying under cover these past few days, Chico. If you love somebody, you don't treat them like this. I'm not ashamed of loving you—are you of me?"

"Come on, baby, you know I'm crazy about you. But I've been married a hell of a long time. I've got a kid . . . Besides, my brothers would kill me if I divorced Betty."

"Okay, but sooner or later it's going to be either her or me. I can't stand sharing you."

Ann Roth was a strikingly beautiful young woman, the kid sister of Lillian Roth, who had played the ingenue in *Animal Crackers*. Ever since visiting Lillian on the set when Ann was only fourteen, she had been infatuated with the ever-charming Chico. Her girlish crush had developed over the years into a conviction that she would ultimately replace Betty as Mrs. Chico Marx. A mutual friend had arranged an introduction, and Chico had instantly fallen for Ann. It was the first time he had ever been deeply moved by any woman other than Betty. Chico arranged the business trip to New York to be near his new love.

My father was a master of deception. It was a relatively simple matter for him to cover up his love affair with Ann Roth, even when Betty's suspicions were aroused. A helpful friend of Betty's had told Chico that Betty was on her way to New York. (Chico wired her flowers in thanks.) So Chico was quite ready for Betty's "surprise" visit.

After Betty's departure, Chico went back to wining

and dining Ann. Ann was pressing Chico to make a firm commitment—was he going to get a divorce and marry her, or wasn't he?

In five days, Chico made up his mind. He wanted Ann.

Chico arrived back in Hollywood without fanfare. He felt that the next few days would change his life. Ann would remain in New York until she heard from him. The problem confronting Chico, however, had no easy solution: Betty, he realized, would not take the news lying down. How was he going to explain to her that he was in love with someone else?

Chico was a singularly selfish man. I doubt whether he ever stopped to consider if he was doing the right thing. Betty had gone through a tremendous amount of hardship for him. If she complained about the extent of his gambling, it was because she was worried about their future. If she had become at times a shrew, he could thank himself for the transformation.

When Chico came home, Betty sensed immediately that something was amiss. Wherever they went, Chico made sure to drag along a friend. They were never alone. Chico stayed out late with cronies. Finally Betty, who couldn't stand the tension anymore, went into his room and cornered him while he was on the phone.

"What's up, honey?" he said.

"You tell me what's up. We haven't had a chance to talk to each other since you got back. Are you in some kind of trouble?"

Chico sat down on the bed and looked away from her.

"Yes," he said, "I guess I am."

Betty didn't know what prompted her, but she asked him, "Is it a woman?"

"Yes," came the reluctant reply.

"Do you want a divorce?" Betty asked.

Chico refused to meet his wife's gaze. Again he answered, "Yes."

Betty was shocked, but she held back the tears. She tried to talk to him.

"Chico," she said, "what makes you think this is going to be easy? I haven't gone through all these years with you just to give you up now without a fight. What's gotten into you? You're crazy if you think Irving [Thalberg] is going to sign you up to a new contract when he finds out how you're treating me." (Mother, of course, really did think all of Hollywood would rally around the wronged wife.)

"Look, Betty . . ."

"In fact," Betty went on, "I doubt whether *anybody* in Hollywood who's the least bit respectable will have anything to do with you."

"I knew you wouldn't understand."

"I understand you perfectly, but you're not getting away with it."

Chico stood up. "I've made up my mind and nothing you can say can make me change it. I'm sorry, but I really love this girl."

"Who? Who are you suddenly in love with?"

"Her name is Ann. Ann Roth."

"Not Lillian's little sister? That little tart has the nerve to break up my home? She's visited us here— She knows you have a wife and daughter. Or have you forgotten about Maxine?"

"Listen, Betty, I have to go out. I'll talk to you later."

"You do that, Mr. Big Shot."

When Chico spoke to his brothers that night, the three of them were incredulous.

"What's got into you, Chico?" Groucho demanded. "Have you lost all your brains to this bitch in New York?"

"If she comes over here," Zeppo said, "I'm not letting her get off the plane."

"You've done enough," Harpo said, making it unanimous. "We've put up with a lot from you over the years, but this is too much."

"That's right," Groucho interrupted. "Betty's too damn good for you. And what do you do? Throw her away. What do you think Irving will say about this? He loves Betty

109

and so does Norma [Shearer]."

Chico left knowing the battle was lost. But still he didn't know what to do. He hadn't thought his brothers would be so opposed to his plans. When he was with Ann, all he could think about was her. But now three thousand miles away from her influence, he wavered.

I found out about the fragile state of our home when Mother walked into my room a few days later. I had felt the extraordinary tensions in the house, but I thought it was probably, as usual, over a gambling debt.

Mother's face was drawn and puffy. "Are you going to sit by while your father breaks up our home?" she said. "Or is it that you just don't care?"

"What in the world are you talking about?"

"Your father wants to leave me for another woman, that's what."

I was stunned. I didn't know what to say.

"Well, are you going to talk to him, or not?"

I walked like a zombie to his room. He was sitting at his desk playing solitaire. I looked at him for a long time, forcing him to speak first.

"What's the matter, honey?"

"I feel awful."

"Why?"

"Because I don't want to live if you leave."

I saw the pain in his eyes. "It's not that bad, honey."

"Worse."

"You really don't want me to go.?"

What did he want me to say? If he wanted me to beg, I would beg.

"I'll kill myself if you go. I'll take poison."

Daddy took me in his arms. "All right, baby. If you don't want me to go, I won't. Can you give me a smile?"

Sure. I knew my cue. The pattern hadn't varied much since their Broadway days when he used my love as an excuse to come back.

Chico stayed home, and things gradually returned to normal. Betty made him call Ann Roth in New York and tell her he wasn't going to see her anymore. She listened in on the other line as her husband fumbled for words to end the affair. Ann hung up in tears.

Betty, however, found it was an empty victory. She still had her husband, but nothing would ever be the same. She knew that Chico had cheated on her for years, but until Ann Roth she hadn't thought there was a chance that anyone could ever take him away from her. She would never be able to believe that again.

As my parents became estranged, I grew bitter. I was convinced that, one way or another, it was all Betty's fault. It didn't help when Mother began to take out her frustrations on me.

"Maxine! What is that? A safety pin? That's you. Her Highness over here. You can't even pick up a needle and thread and sew it. You'll sweet-talk somebody into doing it for you. You're going to sew that right now, and I don't want to see a pin stuck there the next time I see you. I can wear the cheapest dress and make it look good. You always wear the most expensive clothes and you still look like a *schlump*."

My inflection was identical to Mother's, and my savage imitation of this kind of browbeating greatly amused my friends. I was incapable of simply fighting back. If I had, I'm sure she would have stopped her endless needling. Instead, I retreated into meekness and tried to act like the perfect daughter she wanted—at least to her face.

Mother was so strong, tough, self-assured, and beautiful. She seemed to have no chinks in her armor. When she measured me against herself and found me lacking, her angry outbursts intimidated me so much that I shook with rage. Walking quickly, her posture almost overbearing for a woman only five foot two, she looked regal and severe. Harpo called her Napoleon when she was particularly bossy, but she only laughed.

During this period of great stress with Chico, my mother never confided in me. I suppose she thought it wasn't something to speak openly about, but then I gave her absolute-

111

ly no sympathy, even though I didn't know the exact cause of her troubles. As I grew older, I resented it when Mother and I would walk down the street and all the men's eyes were on her. I felt totally inadequate, so I began to lord it over her in another area: education. "Maxine, your hair is all 'aury'"—"Mother that's pronounced 'awry.'" I lifted my eyebrow in disdain when she called from the door, "Maxine, your young swan is here." "Mother," I muttered as I swept out, "It's 'swain,' and nobody uses it today anyway."

Hurt and upset as I was over the break-up, I still played the spoiled little girl with Chico, accepting rewards of ten and twenty dollars every time I rubbed his neck. But something of my real feelings must have come through despite my attempt to hide my deep anxieties. Chico must have sensed I was no longer blithely ignorant of his affairs. One evening, he felt an explanation was in order.

"I'm not very good about women," he said. "You know I like them. And I know how hard it's been on your mother, but I can't help myself. But, baby, believe me when I say that I have never, *never* made a play for an innocent girl."

He was so awkward in describing his feelings that I was moved and gave him a hug. I learned soon enough, however, that it was all baloney. Neither Daddy nor my uncles cared in the least whether or not a girl was a virgin. They would make a pass at anybody, any time, under any conditions.

"I have to feel romantic about a woman before I can get involved," Chico told me.

For Daddy to feel romantic, all he had to do was say hello. And I had seen Harpo in action as well.

Harpo had once taken me on an outing to Catalina Island as a present for my fourteenth birthday. I loved being with him, walking along the sand, hearing his repertoire of show business stories. He told about the time he was late for a matinee because he was stopped by a cop for speeding. (Actually I knew this was Chico's story, but all the brothers swapped lines and parts when it suited them.)

112

"I tried to explain to the officer that I was playing downtown in a show," Harpo recalled, "and that I was late for the matinee. 'I'm one of the Marx Brothers,' I said, 'and if you let me go, I'll give you two free seats.'

" 'I hate the Marx Brothers,' the cop replied, taking out his ticket book.

" 'Well,' I said, 'would your wife like to go? I'll give her the seats.'

" 'My wife hates the Marx Brothers.'

" 'Well, is there anyone in your family who does like us?'

" 'Yeah,' the cop said, pondering. 'I think Aunt Sophie does.'

" 'Great,' I said. 'How about two free seats for Aunt Sophie?'

" 'Not on your life! We hate Aunt Sophie.'

"So he wrote out the ticket, and that's how I was late for the show."

When we were about to return to the mainland on a seaplane, Harpo pointed out a woman to me.

"Do you see that girl down on the beach?"

She wasn't particularly unusual.

"Go over and tell her your Uncle Harpo said there's room on the plane if she'd like to fly back with us."

I thought it odd, but I went over and relayed the invitation. The woman glanced at Harpo, who smiled and waved.

"Sure," she said.

I rejoined him and said that she would be right along. "Who is she?" I asked. "She seems awfully dumb."

"Oh, she's just someone I met once."

When we landed at the airport in Long Beach, we were met by a private car. I sat next to one window, the woman in the center, and Uncle Harpo on the other side. It was a hot day, but Harpo insisted that he and the girl share a lap robe. When he put his hands underneath the robe, the girl started giggling. All the way back to Beverly Hills, he fondled her "under cover."

113

I was really upset. I was very young for my age, and I could easily imagine Chico in a similar situation. He would have done the same thing, though, of course, he wouldn't have used his own daughter as the go-between. If I had told my girl friends about this, they would probably have thought, Well, that's the Marx Brothers for you, as if they were describing some natural phenomenon, like a volcanic eruption, that could be observed but never controlled.

On his way to play cards in the back of a friend's jewelry store, Chico stopped to pick up a newspaper. A policeman on the corner was watching as Chico dug into his grundgy coat for the change. Chico hadn't shaved that morning and snatched the first clothes that he came across so that he wouldn't miss the game. After he bought the paper, Chico found the cop eyeing him suspiciously.

Chico sidled up to him and said, in his best New Yorkese, "Wanna make some money?"

"What are you talking about?" the cop asked with an edge to his voice.

"I'm in the money business," Chico told him, ducking his head furtively. "Cold cash. Today I've got a good buy."

"You better move along, bub," the cop told Chico.

"I'm serious," Chico said, moving closer. "Five dollars is going for $4.25."

The cop looked at him.

"Look. You give me your $4.25, and I'll give you five bucks."

"Get outa here."

"Hey, I tell you what, here's five dollars," Chico said, handing the bewildered cop a five-dollar bill. "Now go into that candy shop over there and get change and then give me back $4.25."

The cop took the bill and got it changed. With some hesitancy, he gave Chico back his part and kept seventy-five cents for himself.

When he finally made it to the card game, Chico told all his friends how he had sold money to a policeman. They egged him on to do a repeat performance for their benefit while they watched from the front of the jewelry store.

So the next day, Chico showed up at the newstand and found the cop there, eyeing him nervously. Chico went over to him.

"I just got today's quotation. Six-fifty going for five bucks."

"You mean if I give you five dollars, you give me $6.50?"

"Absolutely."

"I still don't get it," said the cop, handing over five dollars.

"That's the money market. Some days it's up, some days it's down. You happened to hit an upswing."

Chico gave him $6.50 and walked away whistling.

His cronies couldn't believe it. Much to their amusement, this went on for a whole week. Pretty soon the cop was waiting for Chico to come by—he was hooked.

On the last day of the week, Chico met the cop again.

"Well?" the cop asked, trying to hide his impatience.

Chico shook his head.

"What happened?"

"The market's down." Chico told him. "You have to give me seven bucks for five."

The cop looked relieved. "Oh, is that all!" He handed Chico seven dollars.

Chico refused the money. "My name is Chico Marx. Here's ten dollars—no hard feelings."

"I get it—you're a Marx Brother."

"Right."

"You're nuts, Mr. Marx," the cop said, shaking his

115

head and walking off.

Chico smiled and walked over to his friends in the jewelry store and proceeded to lose considerably more than ten dollars.

The boys finally signed with Irving Thalberg for another two-picture deal. They were happily splitting up the profits from *A Night at the Opera*. Their fifteen percent of the gross had come to a paltry $600,000, but in 1936 that went a long way. That summer they started on a road tour with their new property, *A Day at the Races*.

In San Francisco I spent a full week watching the show take shape, sitting in on all twenty-eight performances. During one evening, when the house was jammed and the audience was having a great time, the show went over its schedule of one hour. There was a particular routine for making transitions: Harpo would come out while Daddy was playing the piano, the two would go into a duet, and then Daddy would leave while Harpo soloed.

To speed things up, the director sent Groucho onstage while Daddy was still playing. Groucho went into his routine, but the audience wanted Chico to continue playing. Unwilling to be run off the stage, Groucho kept right on talking, and the audience began to boo. I don't think that had happened to him very frequently, but he handled the situation with typical skill. He waited until the audience quieted down and then told them, "I have to stay here—I'm getting paid. But nobody's keeping you." They started laughing, and the show was able to go on.

Mother joined Chico and me after one show and we went out for dinner. During the meal, the talk naturally revolved around the new script.

"The show's going to be a hit," Betty told Chico, "but I was just thinking about what's happened to you in all your movies. Every time you have a good gag, the camera's on

116

Groucho. He's always upstaging you. You can't be funny if they can't see you."

"You really think so?" Daddy said, mulling it over. "Well, even if he is, there's not much I can do."

"Of course you can do something. You can assert yourself the next time you boys get together for a story conference."

I saw Daddy was giving the matter serious thought, working himself up to speak to his brothers about it.

The next day, he came home in a rage.

"Betty, don't ever interfere with me and my brothers again! Just remember one thing: There's only room for two prima donnas in the act. Not three. Groucho and Harpo need the limelight. I just need the act to be good."

"I didn't mean any harm," Betty said. "I just thought you deserved better."

"Well, next time keep your ideas to yourself. You almost broke up the Marx Brothers."

Mom and Dad spent the Labor Day weekend in the Monterey peninsula with the Thalbergs and several friends. The group spent the afternoon outside on a veranda huddled over a bridge game. The weather turned cold, and Mother thanked Thalberg when he insisted that she put on his sweater. Betty would always feel guilty for accepting his chivalrous gesture, for Irving came down with a head cold the next day. Lumbar pneumonia eventually set in, and Thalberg died September 14, 1936, still a young man.

A Day at the Races halted production for eight months and then started shooting again. The Marxes weren't optimistic. Their champion at MGM was gone, and in his place stepped the formidable figure of Louis B. Mayer—who detested the Marx Brothers. Chico was especially depressed over the death of his close friend. He felt Thalberg was the only man who ever showed a creative interest in the

117

team—something beyond dollars and cents.

"Our careers will never be the same again," Daddy told me.

A Day at the Races was the last picture the boys made under Thalberg's guidance, and most people would agree that it was their last great film.

Family life had become trying. Daddy was keeping more to himself, and we always had guests for dinner so as to avoid personal matters. Mother was still suffering from the Ann Roth affair, and a chill note crept into her voice whenever she talked to Daddy. To me she was more bossy and brash than ever, and we squabbled endlessly.

This didn't help my confidence much, and I did more daydreaming than was good for me. I was old enough to go out on dates, but boys my age could hardly compare with my imaginary lovers. Dates would press for something more than a good-night kiss on my doorstep, but their advances would only make me feel threatened. I ended up keeping my innocence intact at the expense of gaining some normal experience.

Howie Horowitz, who became a well-known and well-liked television producer, was somebody I instinctively turned to. Arriving in California at the age of seventeen in search of a job in the movie industry, he became a legman for Walter Winchell and hung around the studios all day trying to dig up juicy stories. Howie became a protective brother to me. We shared an obsession with films that bordered on lunacy, and sometimes we would fall in love with a film like *The Scarlet Pimpernel* and see it a dozen times. Daddy soon could boast that I was able to reel off the credits of almost every Hollywood film ever made.

Once Howie took me out to Tarzana in the San Fernando Valley. Zeppo and Marian were giving a party and I was to be included for the first time. When we pulled up to their house, two ferocious Great Danes leaped at the car. Howie and I rolled up the windows and blew the horn until Zeppo came out to save us. "What did he do," Howie asked me in an undertone, "invite us here to get eaten?" Inside, Clark Gable and Carole Lombard were among the guests. Marian, Zeppo's beautiful wife, was one of Lombard's best friends.

I spent the evening sitting entranced before Lombard. Not only was I crazy about her brand of comedy, but I fell in love with her presence and style—and I'm sure Gable felt the same way, as he hardly took his eyes off her all night. Theirs was the most famous romance in Hollywood at the time, but both of them never acted in the least bit phony or self-conscious. Lombard insisted that Clark keep his drinking down because of his weight problem. "We have an agreement," Gable said to me. "I watch my booze and she watches her language." Although Lombard had a notoriously foul mouth, I found her refreshingly frank and open.

I went out with other boys after Howie moved back to New York, and while I wasn't as scared to return their kisses, I missed Howie's friendship. A few weeks after his departure, I received a wire:

MAX'L (his nickname for me)—HURRY!! SCARLET PIMPERNEL AT LOEW'S 83RD. COME RIGHT NOW. CATCH THE LATE SHOW. LOVE HOWIE.

After *A Day at the Races* became a hit, the boys were anxious to get away from Mayer and Metro. Without Thalberg, their filming suffered from what they regarded as the studio's indifference or interference. Sam Wood had directed them a second time, and there was no love lost between him and the team. The brothers were particularly annoyed at the number of takes Wood required to shoot a scene. They felt that by the tenth take a scene had lost its spontaneity. There were endless skirmishes, but both sides tried to keep the set from erupting into open warfare. Only a few people could have bested the boys in verbal duels, and Wood was not one of them.

"You can't make an actor out of clay!" Wood sputtered in anger as the boys were making a mockery of his direction.

"Nor a director out of Wood!" Groucho shot back.

With the money rolling in from *A Day at the Races*, Harpo and Groucho decided that their older brother had better start building up security. Taking over the family's finances, Uncle Groucho put Mother on a budget of $300 a week, while the rest of Daddy's earnings were sent to his broker, Salwyn Shufro. "Hold your seats now, boys," Groucho wrote to Shufro, "here comes the big punch. I'm enclosing a check for Chico, sometimes known as Nick the Greek or Nikko the Chick. By strategy, force, and persuasion, we've withheld this much from him, and this is the beginning of a nest egg for that all-time sucker. Harpo and I will take good care that he doesn't get his mitts on the securities."

They didn't go to such lengths purely for selfless motives. Both Harpo and Groucho were worried that Daddy would one day be a financial burden to them. Neither of his brothers seemed to understand that Chico's incessant gambling was a sickness. Harpo was particularly unsympathetic. He felt that all Daddy had to do was make up his mind to lose a preset amount and then quit, which was Harpo's own approach to betting. Chico's brothers were unwilling to come to grips with the fact that his gambling fever was never going to disappear.

As for Chico, he grumbled about being put on a shoestring salary, but he secretly liked being taken care of. Also, I'm sure he realized that sooner or later Groucho and Harpo would get sick of looking after him and hand over the money.

As part of our new austerity, we moved into a three-bedroom apartment on De Longpre Avenue in West Hollywood. It was located in an apartment complex that resembled Hollywood's version of a large Tudor mansion. Actor Louis Hayward lived in the apartment closest to the street, and I passed his door on my way to our apartment almost every day. He was carrying on a flamboyant affair with Ida Lupino, and Grandma Karp asked me to avoid passing his apartment if I could. She had seen them kissing good-bye several times and thought such lewd behavior needed no audience. I disagreed.

120

Though Mother and Daddy, who had had separate bedrooms at our home in Beverly Hills, had to move back together in the new apartment, our standard of living wasn't drastically affected by Groucho's control, because we continued to have two live-in servants and give dinner parties. Besides, Chico and Betty seemed to have patched things up; she had stopped mentioning other women.

Walter Winchell came to dinner one night, and all of us took an instant dislike to him. He was at the height of his fame and influence, and wasn't too shy to tell us about it. Referring to himself as "we," making authoritative pronouncements, and generally brimming over with spite and gossip, Winchell made an early exit. "That's the problem with this business," Daddy observed after Winchell had left. "That's the kind of bastard who can make or break a career."

One morning I woke up to find Mother and Grandma Karp in a violent argument. They often fought about the same thing. It was only right, reasoned my grandmother, that we, who have so much, should share with those less fortunate. So Grandma would secretly put together a collection of clothes that she didn't think we would miss and then ship it to her poor relatives in Russia. More often than not she was right; the articles would not be missed. If they were, Grandma would simply feign ignorance and go off muttering in Yiddish. A few days earlier, however, Grandma had sent off a pair of Mother's new dress shoes, with rhinestones in the spiked heels. Hardly the proper footwear for tilling the Russian soil.

After the argument, Mother went out to play golf, planning to be home in time for an interview with a reporter from the *Brooklyn Eagle*. She hadn't returned when the woman from the paper arrived, so Daddy and I sat for the interview while Grandma Karp listened.

"We'd like to get an idea of what it's like to live with a Marx Brother," the reporter explained.

Suddenly, Grandma jumped up from behind the piano.

"My son-in-law is a vonderful man. An angel! But mein daughta—"

Both Daddy and I burst out laughing. Grandma was as bewildered as the reporter, but she sensed that she had spoken out of turn, and stopped short.

"You tell her, Ma," Daddy laughed. "Tell her more."

Salwyn Shufro had done such a good job of investing Daddy's money that we were soon able to buy our own house on Elm Drive. Mother was busy working with the interior decorator when Grandma started complaining of pain. Mother quickly rushed her to the hospital. Betty feared the worst since her mother never admitted to being sick. It was discovered that Grandma was in the final stages of terminal cancer. She had evidently suffered considerably without telling anyone.

When I went to see her, I wasn't prepared to find my ever stoical grandmother in agony. "Take me to the ocean and drown me," she said. I felt guilty because I had never taken the trouble to be nice to her. Her penny-pinching ways and old country habits only annoyed and embarrassed me, and for her part Grandma never could understand why I read so much.

She died ten days after being admitted to the hospital. Only recently have I thought deeply about her, and now it's with great sadness. She had been searching, like so many other immigrants, for an easier life. Deserted by her husband, too poor to take care of her two children, and then suddenly in touch with wealth beyond her comprehension, Grandma might well have been living on another planet than on one of the nicest streets in Beverly Hills. The life she understood had died the day she left her Russian *shtetl*. Sitting on her lawn chair, getting some sun, speaking with the family mutt, Trixie, which sat beside her, she felt proud of her son-in-law even though she had never been to one of his pictures.

Mother had to look in the Yellow Pages to find an Orthodox rabbi to officiate at the funeral. As we drove to the cemetery, the rabbi made small talk with Chico about his religious radio broadcasts, boasting of their ratings. Daddy looked over at Mother, but she was crying and wasn't listening to the rabbi's words. But I winked at him.

"You have good ratings, huh?" Daddy said, looking up at the ceiling of the car. "Tell me, do you think you could do a show of broader interest to the Jewish community?"

The rabbi brightened. Now all he wanted to talk about was the possibility of doing a big network show (possibly with the Marx Brothers?). Daddy kept encouraging him, leading him on. He meant no disrespect for Grandma, I'm sure, but he couldn't resist pulling the rabbi's leg.

Back at Elm Drive after the funeral, Mother sat in the dining room, still crying. Harpo and Daddy were impossible. For some reason, whenever they heard Hebrew spoken, it made them laugh. Throughout the service, they made faces at each other and at the rabbi, trying to break each other up. Groucho, who wasn't as close to Grandma Karp as his brothers, was the only one to behave with proper respect. All I needed was to take one look at my father and Harpo, and I started laughing too. I had to run behind the screen in the dining room to keep from breaking up in front of Mother.

Betty came to my room later that evening when I was preparing to go to bed.

"Maxine, your fancy education hasn't taught you how to act like a lady. I'm very disappointed in how you behaved at the funeral today." She tried to sound stern, but her voice cracked in sorrow.

I had nothing to say in my defense. No one had thought to give her the comfort and understanding that she needed. I didn't blame her for being furious with me.

After the service and a brief stopover at the house, Chico had gone off to the race track and lost himself in the excitement of losing.

Betty went to bed alone.

I walked onto the MGM lot a new person—well, almost new. Daddy said I could try to get some bit parts in movies at Metro as long as I didn't neglect schoolwork. Though he was able to arrange a stock studio contract for me, I realized that my being a Marx, while it opened the first few doors, would eventually stand in my way. So I took a new name: Robin Page. It didn't fool anyone.

I was eager to start right away, but although I knew a lot about how Marx Brothers pictures were made, I had no experience when it came to more normal undertakings. *Test Pilot* was being shot, and I decided to see movie-making from a student's point of view.

Myrna Loy and Spencer Tracy were sitting around waiting for the day's shooting to begin. No one noticed me as I slipped onto the darkened set. I quietly took a seat in the rear and got out my pencil and note pad—I was naively determined to get the essentials of screen acting down on paper, before I went in front of a camera myself.

All of a sudden somebody's face loomed over my shoulder.

125

"Shouldn't you be in school, Miss Marx?"

I whirled around to find Clark Gable peering at my "notes."

"Oh, Mr. Gable. I hope you don't mind if I sit in today. I didn't mean to disturb your concentration or anything."

He laughed. "No, I'm just waiting for Fleming [the director] to get the show on the road. What's with the note-taking?"

When I told him, he said, "Yeah, your father mentioned to me something about you wanting to act. He's crazy about you. . . . Well, I better go see how the war is doing."

He started toward the cameras. Then he turned. "Stick with school," he whispered. "Don't let all this," he jerked his head to indicate the sound stage, "go to your head." He winked at me and sauntered to his seat next to the other stars.

What a great guy, I thought. And then I began to giggle. I remembered an incident a few months earlier that made me realize just how human stars can be.

Chico had had an appointment with Dr. Biegelman, an eye doctor who had many of Hollywood's top stars as patients. I went along with Chico as he got an examination and a prescription. As we were about to leave, the doctor mentioned that he had an appointment to see Clark Gable shortly thereafter.

As soon as he heard that, Chico decided to stay. He had a conspiratorial discussion with the doctor.

By the time Gable arrived, Biegelman was nowhere to be seen. Instead, there was Chico, off to one side of the office, wearing the doctor's white coat and headpiece, working on some lenses.

He asked Gable to make himself comfortable in the examination chair. Dimming the lights, he proceeded to put the poor star through the wringer. After having him read from charts that were upside down or sideways, Chico fitted him with lenses that didn't go together. Adding insult to injury, he had Gable get up and bend over so that his head was between his legs, and then scolded him when he wasn't able

126

to read the chart. Daddy then put him through a series of strenuous exercises.

"Why are you doing all this?" Gable finally demanded.

"It's a new technique," said Chico. "Your eyesight has deteriorated so badly, I'm trying to determine what effect your blood pressure has on your vision."

With the doctor's headpiece concealing his face, Chico pressed his forehead against Gable's and shook his head from side to side, clucking sadly.

The actor still didn't suspect anything—but he was getting upset with the doctor, who was both insulting and unsympathetic.

"What's this going to do to my career, doctor?"

"Don't worry, Mr. Gable. It'll be months before you start having real problems."

When Daddy saw that Gable hadn't realized it was a practical joke, he immediately said, "What's the matter, Clark, don't you know me?" He pulled off the headpiece.

"Chico Marx, you bastard!" Gable cried.

I was sure he was going to take a swing at Daddy, who certainly deserved it. But Chico meekly pulled out his own glasses, put them on, and held his palms up.

"You wouldn't hit a man with glasses, would you?"

Finally, Gable fell back into his chair convulsed with laughter.

Now on the *Test Pilot* set, Gable and Tracy were playing a scene in a restaurant. Over coffee, the Tracy character was trying to dissuade Gable from flying that day.

It was fascinating to see how both men worked. Victor Fleming, the director, treated Gable like a robot. "All right, Clark," he would say, "when you hear the line, turn around. Then you pick up the cup. At this word, you set it down." For Tracy, however, Fleming had no suggestions. He just let him come on and read his lines.

Of course, Gable's charisma was there, but he was programmed in every word and action. He trusted the director blindly. I wasn't surprised when Victor Fleming wound up directing *Gone with the Wind.*

My first bit part was as a lady-in-waiting in *Marie Antoinette.* Norma Shearer's behavior during the shooting of the film didn't help my jitters.

Arriving on the set one morning, I smiled and said, "Good morning, Miss Shearer." Although I had been a guest in her home dozens of times, she stared straight through me.

It was Anita Louise, however, who felt the brunt of the star's demands. Anita looked exquisite. Miss Shearer took one look at her and whispered to an assistant director. Anita left the set in tears.

"What's wrong?" I asked her.

"I have to change my costume."

"Why? It's beautiful."

"Miss Shearer doesn't like it. It's too pretty."

Until then, I hadn't really been aware of the star syndrome. Daddy and my uncles were very generous to other performers. But they could afford to be. Nobody could steal a scene from them.

Another day at MGM, I ran into Judy Garland in the ladies' room. She had been crying.

"What's the matter?"

"I'm so ugly," she said.

"You are *not!*"

"Yes, I am. Look at Lana and Annie."

"But they have none of your talent. You're the one who has it all."

"Who cares?" she asked.

When you are a fourteen-year-old kid and your friends are Lana Turner and Ann Rutherford, it could make you feel like an ugly duckling.

Whenever Lana appeared on the set, the gaffers would stop working to gape at her. She was very voluptuous—round yet slender—and her natural coloring was incredible. She had burnished gold hair—this before they made her into a platinum blonde—big blue eyes with dark lashes, and a marvelous complexion.

She was one of the stars in *Dramatic School*, the next picture I had a bit part in. Later, no matter how much I squinted in an attempt to pick myself out of the crowd scenes, I never could. During filming, since I wasn't able to see where the camera was without my glasses, I had decided to stand next to Ona Munson, a featured MGM player. I figured this would get me in some of the shots. But after about the fourth day of shooting, Miss Munson said to me, "Honey, why are you standing next to me? Don't you want to be in the picture?"

"I can't find the camera," I told her. "I can't see."

"You won't find it next to me. The boys know I don't want to be seen."

She explained to me that in order to stay on the studio payroll, she had to report for duty, even though she didn't have a real part. The cameramen kept her out of range so that the audience wouldn't pick her out in a crowd shot.

Paulette Goddard, who was married to Charlie Chaplin at the time, also starred in the picture. Hanging around the set, I noticed her erect bearing—even when relaxing, she sat like a ramrod. "I have to tell you," I told her one day. "I've never seen anybody hold herself like you do. You have the most fantastic posture!"

"So would you," she said, "if you had Charlie behind you with a stick. Everytime I slump, he says, 'Sit up! Sit up!' "

If that was the case, Chaplin was as big a nag as my mother.

Every kid goes through a period of adolescent rebellion, and I was no different. I had begun to realize I was more interested in intellectual matters than my parents were, and I was also developing political attitudes. Not that I could instill them in Daddy, who believed only what he read in the Hearst newspapers. When I tried to explain the dangers of fascism to him, he would reply, "Don't use those *isms* on me!" I would get so angry that tears would come to my eyes.

Chico would turn to Mother in exasperation. *"Sie weint,"* he would inform her—"She cries."

As a child, I had thought my father could do no wrong. Now I began to see him in a more critical light. He was a seducer without conscience who had a basic contempt for women. All the Marx Brothers were the same: They were lechers, the most prominent being my great-uncle, Al Shean. I saw Uncle Al in the movie *San Francisco*, and he looked like a cherub. Some cherub! When he was younger, he and his partner Ed Gallagher were considered the greatest team in vaudeville—and Al regarded every girl in the theater as his *droit du seigneur.*

Age didn't quench Uncle Al's fires. He later appeared on Broadway in *Father Malachy's Miracle.* Visitors backstage were shocked to see the girls in the cast, dressed as nuns, skirts held high, fleeing from the advances of an old man in a priest's outfit. "Don't be unfriendly," he told one. "I just want to fondle your breasts."

Most of the girls that I grew up with had hang-ups about sex, but I was one of the worst. I was afraid that if I ever gave in to my sexual feelings I would end up a female version of my father. Whenever a boy made a pass, I usually laughed at him.

When it came to his daughter, Chico was hardly a libertine. He thought my behavior was exemplary, and the more coolly I handled my dates, the better.

The disparity between my father's expectation that I always remain virginal and his own behavior made a deep impression on me. As a way of fighting for some breathing space of my own, I began to make disparaging remarks about him to some of my friends.

One day, I was walking to my car in the MGM lot and Uncle Harpo called me over.

130

"I want to speak to you, Maxine. Let's go into my dressing room."

He sat me down at his dressing table and stood looking at me. "It's come to my attention," he said, as if he were composing a business letter, "that you've been saying some nasty things about your father in company. Talking about him running after women."

My heart pounded. I had never seen Harpo so angry.

He began to pace around the room. "Whatever you think of him you'd better keep to yourself. I can't stomach disloyalty. And if Chico, who loves you, should hear how you've maligned him, it would break his heart."

He stopped pacing and stared at me. "That's all, but don't ever let me hear of such treachery and ingratitude again."

All the time he had been talking, Harpo had never once raised his voice. He was acting so out of character that what he said shook me much more than if he had ranted and raved. I was so intimidated, it never occurred to me to speak up in my own defense.

I look back on this incident with mixed emotions. I realize how close the Marx Brothers were. Often in their careers they had an "us against them" attitude. Certainly I can see how their mutual regard for one another and their devotion to the act made them intolerant of anyone else's criticism—especially coming from within the family. On the other hand, it had never occurred to Harpo to sit down and talk to me seriously about my father's gambling and women, because Harpo and his brothers were insensitive to the causes of Daddy's problems. Just as Harpo treated Chico's gambling as a simple problem of willpower, so he looked on my actions as simple disloyalty.

Mother arranged my sweet sixteen party at the Cocoanut Grove. I looked terrific. I had gone from a bony 107 to a sleek

115 pounds. Mother gave me one of her long dresses to wear and she stood behind me as I tried it on in the full-length mirror.

"You're just perfect," she said. "Now don't gain any weight!"

It was the wrong thing to say, given the stage I was going through. It was as if she had pressed the wrong button. All my life, I had given away desserts. I hated starchy foods. In the next three months, as if my mother's words had triggered something, I went on a food binge and gained thirty-five pounds. It was a problem that would plague me the rest of my life.

At the party, my friends and I sat at a table with a marvelous ice sculpture centerpiece. As I opened my dinner napkin, a ring studded with diamonds and rubies fell out of it. It was a lovely surprise, and I knew Chico had thought of it. He and Mother sat watching my excitement. They both came over and kissed me.

I knew they wanted the best for me and were even willing to give in to my wish to become an actress. Mother believed that a woman had to be associated with a man to achieve anything. Daddy thought the business was no place for ladies, but he also thought I had a lot of talent, particularly after Eddie Dowling, the well-known Broadway director/producer, had auditioned me and urged Chico to back me in my career.

Miss Barnes, my high school dramatic teacher, had encouraged me. As graduation approached, I sat down to discuss my future with her.

"Who would you advise me to study with?" I asked.

Miss Barnes admired the Stanislavsky Method and knew of a distinguished Russian actress who was a product of the Moscow Art Theatre. Without hesitation, she said, "Maria Ouspenskaya."

The Madame, as she was called, along with Richard Boleslavsky, had founded the American Laboratory Theatre in 1924 to teach the Method. She had recently started her own school.

I wanted to get a second opinion on my drama studies, so I asked an old family friend, Egon Brecher. Czechoslovakian-born, he was the former director of the Eva Le Gallienne Civic Repertory Theater in New York and had doubled as the main character actor of the company.

He shook his head when I brought up Ouspenskaya's name. "She's not right for you, darling. If you had been on stage for many years, and then you went to her, you would perhaps learn something. But for a beginner, or someone who's had a little experience like you, you wouldn't know what to take from her and what to throw away."

In later years, I would be repeating the same advice as a casting director when actors would ask me about studying with Lee Strasberg. For the moment, however, I decided to shelve his suggestion.

I set out for the East Coast to have an interview with Madame Ouspenskaya—before my nerve failed me.

I was frightened when I arrived at her studio for the all-important appointment. Because of her reputation, I expected to find a giant of a woman, but the Madame turned out to be less than five feet tall and tipped the scale, fully clothed in a long peasant dress with many strings of beads, at about 100 pounds.

The rigorous, hostile interview that I had been told she sometimes subjected would-be students to began quietly. The old lady, incessantly smoking, her hair drawn back in a severe bun, looked me over. I thought for a second that she might have established a weight limit for her pupils.

"You want to be an actress," she informed me in a thick Russian accent, sounding very much like the old gypsy she played years later in werewolf movies.

I gulped. "Yes."

"You are willing to work hard?"

"Oh, yes!"

133

"Good. We start in September."
That was the interview.

I may have started to assert my independence, but when I came to New York ready to attend acting school, I was still very much under my parents' domination, even though they were a good three thousand miles away. Mother refused to let me live alone, and so she arranged for me to stay with Aunt Flo and Uncle Mike, who were now living in an apartment on West Ninety-sixth Street.

I left California frazzled from the arguments Mother and I had had over my compulsive eating. It was one fight after another, and it always ended with Mother, slim and elegant, saying, "Why can't you be like me?" Daddy was completely baffled by my ballooning figure. "There's only one exercise, honey," he would say. "You gotta push the plate away from you. I love you no matter how you look. But you're talented. For your own sake, lose the weight."

Now I had at least a semblance of independence. Daddy put me on an allowance of $50 a week for nonessentials. But after Aunt Flo had a talk with Mother on the phone, I found a lock on the breadbox in the kitchen. Talk about the long arm of the law!

I was determined to immerse myself in theater. Maria Ouspenskaya would be my salvation.

It was generally known along Broadway that the Madame was an alcoholic. While appearing in *Dodsworth*, she drank cough syrup when liquor wasn't available. The business manager of the school, who had sobered her up, allowed her to keep her accent as well as her lorgnette, but the beads went.

Madame's approach to acting was highly traditional—technique was everything. The only problem was that none of us in a class of a dozen students had a frame of reference. We would do scenes with interaction and color

134

and nuance, yet we didn't have a well of real-life experiences to draw from.

Classes were held between ten and noon, Mondays, Wednesdays, and Fridays. On Fridays, we were supposed to have a scene prepared for her to critique. The other two days were spent doing improvisations. Once I came to class late and found a girl kneeling on the floor. She got up very slowly. "No, no!" the Madame's voice rang out over the stillness of the room. "I vant you should be playing a half *full* glass of vater."

"But I am, Madame."

"No. You play half empty, my dear."

I did poetic and romantic scenes. I did sophisticated comedies. Anything light and easy. But I couldn't do something suggestively sexual. In one exercise, I was required to play a young girl being subjected to an attack by a venomous older woman. It was impossible for me to show the sensuality of the character.

"Young and passionate girl!" the Madame yelled at me. "You are a young girl. Not old. Young!"

The room we used was immense. The Madame sat enthroned on a huge chair, her tiny feet dangling in space while we performed on the other side of the room. Since I never wore glasses in class, I could barely make out the blur of her chair from that distance.

One of my big moments came when I was playing the daughter in *Mourning Becomes Electra*. I put everything I had into the role—it was a big dramatic scene. Halfway through, I stopped short. Somebody was snoring. I couldn't see who it was.

"I am so sorry, Maxine, but you've put me asleep," the Madame said.

After class, a friend told me that the Madame had first pantomimed going to sleep for a few minutes, and it was only when she saw I hadn't noticed her that she had begun to snore.

In the middle of the term, Madame informed us she would be leaving school for a few weeks to make a picture in Hollywood. I called Daddy excitedly. "My teacher's coming

135

to California. You've got to take her out. Somewhere nice!"

Later, Chico reported back that he had accomplished the mission. "We took her to the Mocambo. I did my best to entertain her. I ever danced with her for a while. But she dances very peculiarly. She sort of hopped up and down."

When she returned to New York, Madame approached me after class, looking puzzled.

"Maxine," she said, "it was nice of your father to take me out dancing. But why did he jump up and down like little sparrow?"

With my good friend Toby Ruby living in New York, I hardly ever had a dull hour. After school we would meet and go to the Capitol Theater before one o'clock and get in for a quarter. It was forbidden to bring food into the theater, but we smuggled in huge delicatessen sandwiches. The usher, drawn by the smell of dill pickles, would check the area around us, row by row. Hiding our paper bags, our mouths full, we would shake our heads in pop-eyed innocence.

Mitzi Green was headlining at a big movie house when Toby and I went to see her. Mitzi's mother, Rose, was aptly named, for she could have been the original Mama Rose of *Gypsy* (a role that Mitzi would triumphantly play in years to come).

We went backstage to renew our friendship with Mitzi and ran into Rosie. After the hellos, she asked, "Did you see the soft pink spot they put on us? They made us look awful."

"I'm dying to see Mitzi," I told her. "How is she?"

"Our throat is very bad today," Rosie replied.

Mitzi was delighted to see Toby and me. "We have to be back by the five o'clock show," Rosie instructed her daughter. Mitzi just shook her head.

I returned to Hollywood that summer with a feeling of new energy. Not only was I more of a "professional," but I knew the break away from home life had done me good.

Egon Brecher spent a few hours each week giving me instruction in acting. He tried to get me to burst through my inhibitions by making me roar Shakespearean sonnets "as if I were a lion in a garden." Chico didn't know quite what to make of these lessons, but he seemed impressed by my energy and devotion.

I was beginning to perfect my skill with accents. It was easy for me to mimic the Russian intonation and word placement of Gregory Ratoff. He had often enough said to me at dinner, "Hello, Maxine, I am so good to see you."

I could do Irish, French, Austrian, and Cockney. Of the latter, English people would swear that it was a perfect Australian accent. But it was all relative.

"In a play I did in Vienna," Brecher told me once, "I played a Japanese. On stage, I was playing beside six real Japanese. The next day, one paper said that I was the only convincing Japanese in the cast. It was true. I played the Austrian idea of a Japanese."

I was roaring a sonnet one morning when Chico came to me with a strange suggestion.

"Honey, I've been thinking," he said. "I think it's about time you had a dog."

"What?"

"Sure. Every child ought to have a dog."

"But I'm not a child. I'm seventeen. Why do you think I suddenly want a dog, Pop?"

"I think it should be a big dog," Chico went on. "Maybe a German shepherd or a Doberman pinscher."

"But Daddy, a Doberman can be vicious."

"Yes, that's true. But they make excellent guard dogs, as well as loyal pets. A Doberman . . . that's it."

Chico persisted all day in selling me on how wonderful the relationship between a girl and her Doberman could be.

I finally went to Mother to find out if she knew what his sudden absorption in canines was all about.

"He's scared to death of gangsters," she said. "He probably owes them a lot of money and feels he needs some protection. Just ignore him."

Chico seemed to drop the idea for a couple of days, when one afternoon he ushered in a vicious-looking white pit bull. "This is Charlie," he said. "Charlie's a great dog and we're already great pals."

Unfortunately, Charlie turned out to have the sweetest disposition I have ever seen in an animal. He wouldn't bite intruders. He'd lick them to death.

Chico was perennially in fear of the mob, but loath to admit it. "They're not bad guys," he would mutter. But he usually managed to be out of town whenever he owed money.

I was taken on at the Pasadena Playhouse that summer. In the production of *Night Over Taos*, by Maxwell Anderson, I was cast as an old peasant.

The young villain was played by Preston McServey, who, with his future wife, Cathy, was a full-time student at the Playhouse.

"There's a kid out here you should look at," I told Zeppo. "I think he's got picture possibilities."

"What's his name?"

"Preston McServey."

"Now that's a name," he laughed. "What am I going to do with an unknown kid?"

138

A year later, I was in Zeppo's office when he asked, "Say, Maxine, what's the name of that guy who was at the Playhouse with you?"

"Preston McServey."

"Maybe I ought to take a look at him."

"It's a little late. Cecil B. DeMille saw him and put him in a picture called *Union Pacific*. He's changed his name to Robert Preston."

My next role at the Playhouse came when I won an open audition for the part of the ingenue in *The Old Maid*. Since it was my first leading role, the Marx Brothers turned out for the opening. I was more nervous performing before those five than for the entire audience. They worshipped success.

After the show, Daddy was the first to come backstage to greet me.

"You were tops, baby! I wonder where you got it from?"

"Where else, Dad, but from you."

"I never played a straight role in my life. You were great!"

When Groucho came over I could tell a wisecrack was coming. "Which one of you was the ingenue?" he said, referring to the sensitive young man who played my love interest. Well, I thought, what do you expect from Groucho?

Zeppo and Aunt Marian had brought over one of their clients, Barbara Stanwyck, as a guest. Her career had been going down the drain when Zeppo, as her agent, got *Stella Dallas* for her, and she was a bigger star than ever.

Miss Stanwyck was direct and personal. "Now listen to me," she said. "Anybody with your talent who doesn't get thin should be ashamed of herself. I weighed a hundred and forty pounds when I came to Hollywood. I literally starved myself. There's no excuse for you. I didn't have your ability."

Of course, I weighed 145 pounds at the time, and I was grateful to her, but I felt it would take more than words, no matter how encouraging, to overcome my problem.

The Los Angeles Times reviewer made my day: Little Miss Maxine Marx revealed a delicate charm and unusual style and variety in her beautifully nuanced playing of the young daughter."

I choose to ignore the wise guy who reviewed me in another paper as giving "a nice, buxom performance."

In a short time I was back in New York for my second and last year of dramatic school. I finished the year with a letter from Madame Ouspenskaya praising my work for being "simple, direct, and highly effective."

My career seemed to be picking up just as Chico was losing interest in his. The Marx Brothers were discontented with the way their movies were turning out. All of them worried that they were rapidly becoming repetitive and uninspired. *Room Service* and *At the Circus*, while not totally without redeeming bits and pieces, were simply not up to their previous standards. The only happy experience from this period right before the war was the tour of *Go West*.

I would get up in the morning and go with Chico to the theater, sitting through the four shows every day. The morning audience usually consisted of a few drunks and whores, a stranded tourist or two, and me. The quality and quantity of the crowd improved as the day went on.

On the fifth day of the tour, as the weekend approached, I decided to have my hair done. The first show was a good time to go to the beauty parlor.

I arrived backstage after the show, where Harpo and Daddy were impatiently waiting for me.

"Well?" Chico asked.

"Well what?"

"I told you she wouldn't know," Harpo said.

"Know what?"

"We switched parts," Chico said, "and you never guessed. I was sure you'd guess."

140

My heart sank. "Maybe I would have guessed, but I wasn't in the audience."

They were like two kids whose party had been spoiled and I felt the same way. I knew they would never repeat the switch again.

Once Chico came with me to an audition for a screen test and offered to read with me since no one else was available. We had a scene from a light comedy, but it was too big a "stretch" for Chico. Chico's line was "Where do you think you're going?" Peering nearsightedly at the script, he spoke, " 'Where—' Wait a minute, here—Oh, yeah, 'Where-do-you—' Ah, 'Where-do-you-think-you-are-going?' "

"Pop! Read it the right way!"

The casting director stopped the scene after Chico had stumbled through a few more lines. He said, "Well, Chico, you nearly ruined it for the kid."

I succeeded in getting a screen test (silent—the talent scout had complimented me on my reading, yet they gave me a silent test) at Twentieth Century-Fox, but nothing came of it. Common sense dictated that I would have to work hard to become an accomplished performer. I would also have to lose weight. But in my imagination I was already a big star.

A girl friend of mine, Bobbie, came to visit me while she was in California. We had known one another at Woodmere Academy. She was a psychology major in college and was eager to hear about my troubles—particularly my tendency to live in a fantasy world.

"I think I must be a schizophrenic," I confided.

"That depends," Bobbie said. "Do you prefer to go out and have a good time, or would you rather stay home and fantasize?"

"I guess I'd rather go out."

"Then you're not a schizophrenic," she assured me.

Bobbie, it turned out, had some rather strong fantasies of her own. She was a confirmed star worshipper.

141

From the very first day at our house, she seemed to have eyes for no one else but Chico.

Bobbie tried everything she could to make a good impression on him. She would get up early in the morning and the two would go off for a swim before Mother and I awoke.

Then one day the storm broke in full force. Bobbie came to me in tears—or a good imitation of them.

"What's wrong, Bobbie?" I already sensed that I wasn't going to like her answer.

"It's Chico . . . I hate to tell you this, but your father made a play for me last night. He slipped into my room. I had no idea he felt that way about me!"

I was too upset to see that she was bragging.

"Please, Maxine, don't get upset. It's nothing really; I'll get over it eventually. Honest."

Bobbie walked out of the room. I could have killed her. She had known about Chico's reputation; she had probably counted on it.

Mother had once threatened that if Chico ever tried anything with someone under her roof, she would never forgive him. I remembered that, yet something compelled me to run into her room and, with a rush of words, tell her everything.

When I had finished, Betty looked at me almost blankly—as if she were feeling nothing.

"That does it. That's the one thing I swore I'd never put up with from him. I'll see to Chico, but first get that bitch out of my house—she's no friend of yours."

Mother stayed in her room most of the day. When she came out, she went directly to Chico's bedroom. I could hear his angry voice raised in what would be their last big conflict. "Okay, I admit it. But I didn't do anything that she didn't encourage."

"That's hardly an excuse! Anyway, I've had it with you and your excuses. I'm through, finished."

Perhaps she waited for a sign from Chico, some word that might spark a reconciliation, but none was forthcoming. I don't doubt that they both still loved each other. But when

142

my mother went back to her room, I knew something irreparable had been done to their marriage.

From that point on, Chico lived under the same roof with us but was no longer part of the family. He took no meals with us. He would get up in the morning and have breakfast, then leave for the day, coming home to change before going out again for dinner. If he wanted to speak to me, he would ring a bell in his room that sounded downstairs, and I would go up and see what he wanted.

I'm sure that both of my parents thought they would patch up their differences eventually, but the agony went on for years. Of course I felt guilty—I had precipitated the disaster. But I also felt strangely relieved. The worst had happened, and now a kind of shell-shocked calm pervaded the house.

The situation was not without its bitter humor. One night, Arthur Gordon (of Marx and Gordoni fame) was having dinner with Mother and me when we heard a door slam in another part of the house.

"What was that?" Arthur asked.

Mother replied with a faint smile, "It's the phantom of Elm Drive."

World events would shortly be tearing millions of families apart. We Marxes were torn apart without any outside interference.

Aunt Ruth, who had long been miserable under Groucho's constant cascade of insults, demanded and got a divorce. Ruth's alcoholism had been out of control for some time, and I think Groucho was glad to get rid of her. He had no sympathy for anyone who showed weakness.

Mother was taking her separation from Chico very well. By this time, she had her own life in Hollywood, her own friends, and her own amusements. I knew she was still in love with Daddy, but any reconciliation was impossible since Chico was never going to make any fundamental changes in his life.

"The one thing I'm glad about is that I insisted the house be listed in my name," Mother said. "I own it. Otherwise I wouldn't be able to sleep nights worrying that Chico would sell it right out from under us." She wasn't exaggerating, either. Chico's gambling had stepped up ever since Mother and he had severed daily relations. There wasn't anyone around now to hold him, however loosely, in check.

145

The Marx Brothers' last picture at MGM, *The Big Store*, was another letdown for the aging team. It was much worse than *Go West*, which had at least a couple of funny scenes. Chico was a determinedly optimistic high roller who needed the big money that came in from studio contracts to support his carefree lifestyle, but now, in 1941, the Marx Brothers were at their lowest ebb. Neither MGM nor RKO or, for that matter, any film company, wanted to have a team of washed-up comedians on its payroll. At least that's how Uncle Groucho put it. He never romanticized their setbacks. He felt that they were indeed past their collective prime.

Yet, because he was desperately in need of income, Chico couldn't afford to sit back and leisurely decide what would be the best course. The eldest of the brothers, without any money in the bank and missing the psychological support that home life had always offered, had to keep busy. Unlike Groucho and Harpo, who had saved their money all their lives, my father was forced to spend his last two decades as an entertainer—for hire.

I had never seriously believed the brothers' oft-repeated threats to retire. Now I saw that all were serious about no longer making pictures. Their days as a team were over. This hit home when I learned from Mother that Chico had gone to New York to work as a bandleader. His separation from Mother, theoretical as long as they continued to live under the same roof, became factual. The split came one year before their silver wedding anniversary.

When Groucho saw that Chico and Betty were not going to get together again, he came over to see Mother. Groucho walked into the living room, and before Betty could say hello he tossed a flat envelope in her lap.

"Here's the money we managed to save before Chico had a chance to squander it. There's nearly $300,000 there in securities. Your husband is a confirmed bum, and I don't want to have anything to do with taking care of him anymore. You give him what you think he deserves."

At my mother's pained expression, Groucho walked over to where she was sitting and touched her hand. "I'm

146

sorry about this, Betty, but . . . well, I know that you had to put up with a lot of hard times with that louse. . . . I have to go now. See you sometime."

"I knew that, deep down, Groucho meant well, but he had a funny way of showing it. Hearing him put down Chico didn't console me," Betty later recalled. "I was still in love with Chico. I didn't want to hear bad things about him from Groucho."

Groucho was basically a decent man. He realized that if he simply handed the money over to his brother, Betty wouldn't see any of it. But he had handled the whole affair badly.

"I didn't care to listen to criticism of Chico—a man who, whatever else you have to say about him, was full of love inside him," Mother said. "I don't doubt that, until he died, Chico still loved me. And for my part, I never regretted marrying him. Perhaps I should have let go sooner, but . . ." Her voice trailed off.

Groucho, I suppose, was embarrassed about getting involved in the first place. He wrote Mother a letter shortly after his visit. In it he said he was sorry that he had been so abrupt at their meeting, and that he hadn't meant to be. But then, almost perversely, Groucho started right in again denigrating Chico. At the end of his diatribe, he gallantly pointed out that all Betty would have to do in order to get a divorce would be to show a judge what he, Groucho, had written.

There was an underlying difference in Chico and Groucho's failed marriages. Drunk and ruined, Ruth ended up detesting her former husband, while Mother still wanted to defend Chico's good name. It must have been extremely hard on Groucho to see how easily Chico attracted loving women—first Minnie and later Betty. This fact and Chico's flagrant disregard for money confused and troubled Groucho. He couldn't help but be jealous of this man who never seemed to "earn" the loyalty he received.

It was a highly complex love/hate relationship between the two brothers. As can be seen from a letter Groucho

147

wrote to his long-time personal friend, Dr. Samuel Salinger in March 1942, Groucho did not know quite what to praise or condemn in Chico:

> *He is a diminutive, dynamic combination of Ponzi and Casanova, who disregards all the laws of life and constantly snaps his fingers in Fate's kisser—he gambles with everything—but who knows, maybe he has the right idea?*

True to form, when Betty gave Chico half of the invested securities, it took him all of three months to blow it. At present, Mother is still living in comfort from her share.

Band life attracted Chico. The schedule was tough, of course, being reminiscent of the old vaudeville one-night stands, but Chico found that his name packed the house every night. The band was a good vehicle for his talents. He would come on stage, tell a joke or two, and then introduce the show. During the course of the program, he would shuffle toward the center spotlight, pretend to conduct the band, tell a few more jokes, take out a banana and start to eat it, and wind up with a solo number. The solo was what the audience generally waited around for, and they loved it: ten unadulterated minutes of Chico shooting the keys and singing the old songs.

Chico, in an article he wrote for *Billboard*, recalled some of his anxieties about performing without his brothers. It was typical of him that he made light of his opening-night worries:

> *We began our tour at the Flatbush, Brooklyn, which is known for having the toughest audience in that part of the country . . . Every fifteen seconds I'd think I was hearing Harpo blowing that*

*automobile horn, and every other fifteen seconds
I'd wish he was.*

Some things hadn't changed, though. While Chico was on the road, his reputation as a ladies' man preceded him to such an extent that when he reached New York to play at the Roxy Theatre, Gae Foster, the director of the theater's chorus line, posted a sign backstage: "Any Girl Found on Chico Marx's Floor Will Be Immediately Fired!"

The warning must have lifted Daddy's spirits.

Now that Chico was gone, living with Mother at the house on Elm Drive became monotonous. I still longed to break into show business in a big way, but it seemed that the studios had not yet gotten the message. I was up to my ears in crowd scenes, and although I was paid for my day's work, the professional satisfaction was nil. Movies were, for the moment at least, a dead end. So I decided to move to New York to look for stage work.

Ray Milland was a neighbor of ours in Hollywood, and occasionally I would go next door to play with his adorable two-year-old son. The actor would usually be around reading the paper. Before I left for the East Coast, I asked him if he knew anybody in New York who could give me a job. Milland said he would be going there shortly himself, and that I should look him up.

I called him the day he arrived, and the next night he called back, around eleven.

"How about meeting me for a sandwich?"

"Sure!"

"Okay, meet me at Reuben's."

I dressed quickly.

His call had flattered and titillated me. The girl that I wanted to be desired a midnight rendezvous with a star. The

149

real Maxine, naive and frightened, had a hard time forgetting that Milland was an older man and married to boot.

As we chatted, however, I got the distinct impression he didn't think I was so innocent.

He reached over and stroked my hand during our conversation. I managed to hide my confusion by lighting a cigarette.

"You know, Maxine, I've been noticing you for a long time now. You're a very pretty girl."

I couldn't believe he was making a play for me. But then the columns had suggested that he was having trouble with his wife.

"Why don't we go to my place? I have a terrific view of the East River."

I was trembling inside, but the worldly Hollywood sophisticate I was pretending to be took over for me. "Why not?" I heard myself reply breezily.

When we reached his apartment, he turned the lights low. He started to kiss me, softly but firmly, and I loved it. I kissed him back.

He led me slowly into the next room, which turned out to be the bedroom. I felt myself becoming nervous. The moment he suggested that I take off my dress, the Hollywood sophisticate vanished and I started to cry.

I hadn't wanted the courting scene to end. It all fit into my romantic fantasies. However, sex was a reality that I didn't want to have to deal with.

Milland immediately saw he had made a mistake. His face registered neither surprise nor anger.

"Come on, honey," he said gently, taking me by the arm. "I'll take you home."

The weeks slipped by and my routine hardly varied. I was having absolutely no luck in getting a job. I would walk miles each day between casting sessions, and I had nothing to show for my effort but blisters. I began to be known around town as the girl with the shoes on her back. My feet couldn't take heels for very long periods of time, so I went from office to office in sensible walking shoes, with a pair of heels in a bag slung over my shoulder. Just before entering an office, I would do a Clark Kent number in a phone booth and come out wearing high heels.

I wanted to get into a new George Kaufman–Moss Hart show, but heard that Arlene Francis had already been signed for the part I was after.

I asked Kaufman if I could read for the understudy.

"No," he said, "you're too young."

Sitting in Sam Harris' office, I could hear Kaufman and Hart talking behind closed doors. Mr. Harris came out. He knew I had been waiting there a long time.

"How long are you going to sit here, Maxine?"

I was sick of *schlepping* around all over town and always being a fraction too late, or not being quite what they were after. "Until I speak to Mr. Kaufman again," I said, "or get older."

Mr. Harris shook his head. "Minnie's child . . . you'll make it."

But not, as it turned out, in the Kaufman–Hart show.

One day Margaret Dumont, who had returned to New York after her stint in Marx Brothers' movies ended, called me out of the blue and we arranged a lunch date.

She arrived at the restaurant wearing white gloves up to the elbow and carrying a lorgnette. During the meal, Miss Dumont talked about how the Marx Brothers had affected her life.

"The boys r-r-r-ruined my car-r-r-r-eer-r," she trilled.

"How, Miss Dumont?"

"Oh, my dear. Nobody took me seriously as a dramatic actress. People always thought they saw Groucho peeking out from behind my skirt."

I felt sad. She never realized what a great foil she had been and how much she had contributed to their movies. She was notorious for being without sense of humor. The boys

151

could never break her up because she never thought they were funny.

Times were tough for Chico. He refused to trim his style of living to suit his cut in salary. Too many years of doing exactly what he wanted were taking their toll on him physically as well. He was beginning to have pains in his chest, which scared him a little. He was finding it harder to stay up all night playing poker and then do a show the next day.

I wrote him that I was worried about his health. I had heard from a number of people that he wasn't taking care of himself. In reply, he wrote,

Dear Maxine:

Your letter of three days ago reached me and you know that I was very glad to get it. Just opened in Portland and everything went wrong with the first show. The mikes didn't work, the piano was no good, some of the musicians' instruments were injured in transit, my dressing room cot is broken, the weather was threatening, the food stinks, the audience is few—otherwise everything is fine.

Do not worry about the previous paragraph, it was meant to be funny.

I have been feeling better but at times not quite like my old self. It is just that I need a little rest and I may go up to the country for four days in the mountains next week if I get a chance.

You must not believe what you hear because people are only too happy to bring you news that will make you unhappy. It's a human trait.

I am enclosing a money order for you for $100 which will take care of your spring coat and, if necessary, a new hat. Also a little money for your purse . . .

Maybe sometimes I wish I had just saved a bit more money. But I got a oil well and I'm drawing $1.80 from it every month. Steady. I guess there's time to make a fortune yet.

Your loving Daddy,
Chico

I hadn't mentioned in my letter that I had heard something else. A friend of the family told me that Chico had gotten pretty serious about an actress he had met some years ago whose name was Mary Dee. When I questioned Mother about this new development, she assured me she knew all about Mary. I was surprised to hear how bitter she sounded, but I soon learned one reason was that Mary Dee was a good twenty years younger than Mother. Friends who had seen Chico and Mary together also told me how much she and Betty resembled one another. I suppose Mother had heard this, too. Such a comparison could not have pleased her.

I got another letter from the wandering Chico a few weeks later.

Dear Baby:
Opened at the Orpheum yesterday and the show went over very well. Business was good considering that we are having zoot-suit riots here and the radio keeps urging people to keep off the streets downtown. Naturally, that doesn't help. Was in San Diego last week and broke the house record for all time.

I feel better this morning than I have in a week or so but am having another X-ray at the hospital tomorrow as I get attacks quite frequently in my chest. So far, they can't quite determine the cause but hope to get me straightened out soon.

Love,
Daddy

I decided to see for myself if Chico was all right.
I took a train to Chicago, where Chico was playing at

153

the Orpheum Theatre. His hotel suite had a living room and a bedroom. Chico said I could take the living room to save on expenses. He seemed happy to see me and looked in good shape, except for a few more wrinkles around his eyes. I hadn't been alone with him for ages, but now we would have a week to ourselves.

"It must bring back the old memories, Pop, all this staying in hotel rooms and travelling nonstop."

"Yeah. I'm pretty tired of it," Chico said. But then his face brightened. "It's kind of fun, though, still being able to sit down at the piano and get a few laughs. Thank God they still laugh!"

I don't think my father resented having to scrape by while his other brothers sat on their millions. He knew he had dug his own hole, and I was proud of him for going out on the road and making his own way.

As I was putting my clothes away, I discovered a girdle in one of the drawers. I took it into him, holding it between two fingers.

"Whose is this?"

Chico looked at me with a perfectly straight face. "It must be the maid's."

We stood looking at each other. Then we both started laughing.

After a while, Chico told me about Mary Dee. I hadn't realized what a permanent part of his life she had become. Mary's hold on him was very strong. Chico, after all, was twice Mary's age, and he was scared of losing her.

My guess was that she wasn't far from our hotel, waiting for me to leave.

For the moment, though, I had Daddy all to myself. We would take a cab to the theater at noon every day, and Chico would always tell the driver to stop at a particular corner. Getting out of the cab, he would say to me, "Wait a minute. I'm going for some cigarettes." He would disappear into a cigar store and then come out five minutes later. It took me three days to see the pattern.

154

"Is your bookie in there?" I asked finally.

Chico looked startled. He expected that from Mother, not from me. Grinning, he said "How do you think I make the money to pay for your dinner? They're really small bets . . . just enough to pay for cabs and dinners and such."

I was touched to hear how broke he was. It was difficult for him to play it safe by betting small. He was assured of making money if he wanted to. He knew how to play the odds. During my stay, he was content to make twenty or thirty dollars a day. We ate at all the places he loved, and he paid cash.

One night between shows, radio's Quiz Kids came backstage to see him. One of the kids was a mathematical genius. "Give me a dollar bill," Chico told the boy. The youngster handed one over. Chico glanced at it and gave it back, proceeding to recite the serial numbers forward, backwards, and from the middle out. "If you want to hold on-to that bill and call me in a year," Chico told the wide-eyed boy, "I'll tell you the numbers again. If not, I'll forget them tomorrow."

His memory was incredible. Naturally, he made a game out of it.

Mother's voice was shrill as she argued with me.

"Chico, Chico, Chico. One day you'll take my side for once. What do you mean *I* should try to understand? Why don't you ever try to understand me? I didn't desert you. Who's pretending she doesn't exist, anyway? I never said that. I just want to know why I have to talk about her or listen to you talk about her in my home!"

Mother and I didn't quite see eye to eye on the subject of Mary Dee. I thought she should face the facts and realize that there was someone else in Chico's life. Mother thought I was betraying her. Not that she wished to have Chico back.

Betty just didn't like to think of him with anyone else

"I'll tell you one thing, young lady," she said. "I don't want you to see your father when that woman is around. You're my daughter and you'll do as I say as long as I'm supporting you."

"Look, Mom, I don't like the idea of Chico seeing Mary any more than you do, but he's not going to stop seeing her if I don't visit."

It took Mother a long time to finally accept the situation for what it was. For the next fifteen years, whenever Chico paid us a visit, she would ask him if he wanted a divorce.

He would look at me. "I didn't hear anything, did you?"

"I said, 'Do you want a divorce?' " Mother would repeat.

"I never heard a word she said," he would tell me.

Mother would drop the subject until his next visit or phone call, and they would go through the same routine. Eventually Chico began to make excuses for not seeing me.

One day I couldn't take it any longer and called him. "I'm coming over to see how you are," I told him.

"Well, I'd love to see you, baby, but I have this poker game and . . ." I ignored the fake excuse and told him I was coming over.

The dinner itself was pretty awkward. Mary and I had very little to say to each other. She was dark and tiny waisted and I could see how people might have thought she resembled Mother. I was to discover a far closer similarity. Both women were extraordinarily loyal and loving. When Daddy started to get sick, Mary stayed by his side for years and nursed him.

After the evening with them, I told Mother what I had done. She was furious.

"Well," she said, "now you've put your sanction on their relationship!"

"Mother, that's nonsense! I want to be able to see my father. It's as simple as that."

For once, I had the last word.

Chico had his reasons for not divorcing Mother. I'm sure it was because he didn't want an actual, irrevocable

156

break with the family. Mary wanted to get married and Chico convinced her it was Betty's fault for not giving him a divorce. Mother settled the issue herself in 1959 by deciding to remarry. Only then, more than two decades after their separation, was Chico "free" to marry Mary.

While Mother went on a trip to New York, I decided to stay on in California at Uncle Groucho's house. I was in a bad way emotionally. I was twenty years old, but I already felt disillusioned about making it in the theater.

Uncle Groucho's was not exactly the best place for me at the time.

In those days, Groucho wasn't much given to displays of wealth. Some twenty-five years later, when I visited the house he had built for his third wife, Eden, in Trousdale Estates, I was amazed by what his last companion, Erin Fleming, had accomplished. She had turned a skinflint into a spendthrift. He had round-the-clock nurses, cooks, and housekeepers, a secretary, and a gardener. He even had hired a young man to come in on Fridays and run films for him in the projection room. Groucho hosted dinner parties several times a week, and the lavish food was a far cry from the skimpy fare served in the past. Caterers were called in for large-scale entertaining, such as his annual *seders*, his birthday parties, or receptions to celebrate the publication of a new book.

This wasn't the man I knew. His large house in Hillcrest, where I had stayed in the past, was cheaply furnished, unattractive, and tacky. When he had been married to Aunt Ruth, I knew he didn't let her have a say in running the house. Yet even though he did the marketing himself, he loved nothing better than to complain about his wife's choice of food to his guests.

I can remember one evening at their house when Chico and Mother were still together. We sat down and the soup was served. "I bet the soup is better in a concentration camp." Groucho said to us, not looking at Ruth. He kept it up at every course. "If there are any gourmets at the table, speak up now

157

or forever hold your tongue," Groucho intoned. All of us were laughing except Ruth. Groucho had actually done everything for the meal but cook it, and she was being blamed. He had even hired the cook!

At the outset of my stay, Groucho made me feel totally unwelcome. He had no interest in my problems. In fact, he made it a point to tell me just about every day how much he disapproved of "moochers" and "loafers." If I was aimless and unhappy, all the more reason I should stay out of his way. I had always been friendly with his daughter, Miriam, and I pitied her for having such an ogre for a father.

Groucho had years ago felt that I was a good influence on Miriam, who was a little hell-raiser. When Miriam was younger, she had no fear of her father, and was almost contemptuous of him, much to Groucho's amusement. The more she mocked him, the higher she would rise in his esteem. But now, at the age of fifteen, Miriam seemed beaten down, intimidated.

All that summer, I often felt the same way. His divorce and the breaking up of the brothers' act had left Groucho in a permanently foul mood. I spent three months there sneaking past his room so that he wouldn't subject me to one of his caustic lectures on the value of hard work.

Miriam and I would wake up in the morning in adjoining rooms. Scurrying into mine, she would ask in a whisper, "Is Daddy awake?"

"I don't know."

"Well, go look," she would say, trying to urge me out of bed.

"Why should I look? He's *your* father. You go."

"Go on. Please. He won't yell at you."

"Why not?"

She would never have a good answer to that one. Groucho didn't need an excuse. Now I can't believe how a man who so genuinely loved his children, as Groucho did, could almost deliberately drive them away. A genius with the fast putdown, he was tongue-tied when it came to expressing even the simplest tender feeling.

158

If you were weak, he could be brutal.

The look in Miriam's eyes told me everything. "He wants to speak with you," she said to me one day.

"Can you tell me what about?"

She shook her head. "He's in his bedroom."

When I walked into Groucho's room, he was waiting for me.

"There's no more money," he said. Although he had been housing and feeding me, I hadn't asked him for any spending money, being content with the weekly allowance Chico sent.

"What do you mean, Uncle Groucho?"

"Your father's broke. You won't be getting any more money from him."

"I see."

He turned his back on me and went over to his closet. "That's all, Maxine," he said.

Groucho didn't think that the news about Chico being in trouble would distress me. When I didn't say anything to Miriam, she asked me later what Groucho had wanted. I couldn't answer her for fear that I wouldn't be able to control my anger and humiliation.

I was still at Groucho's in early October when his birthday rolled around, and so I went to one of the better men's shops and bought him three expensive neckties. When he opened my present, he took a look at the ties and threw them at me.

"I never wear this kind of tie."

I ran into the kitchen, crying.

His current girl friend lit into him. "Of all the despicable things to do! How could you?"

Chastened somewhat, Groucho called to me. Blowing my nose and wiping my eyes, I returned to the breakfast room. He struggled with himself a bit and finally said, "You better return these things. Thanks for thinking of me."

When faced with sentiment or emotion, Groucho retreated into the behavior associated with his nickname. But I was too young to rationalize.

159

Mother arrived a week or so later, and for once I was happy to be under her wing. If anybody could stand up to Groucho, she could.

Mother didn't waste any words with me. "I want you packed and ready to leave immediately."

"Why the rush?" I asked.

"Because your Uncle said some terrible things about you that no one has a right to say. So I gave him a piece of my mind and now I've come to get you out of here."

"What did he say?"

"He said you were lazy . . . that you were a parasite. I don't know, stupid things . . . like that you were a bad influence on Miriam."

"He said that?"

"And worse. Come on, let's go." Mother burst into tears. I had seen her cry only a few times in my life.

How could he have said those things? I had tried my best to make myself agreeable. I always cleaned my room and helped out around the house. I was baffled.

Groucho succeeded in driving me away—just as he did most of those close to him. His brothers were the only people who weren't frightened of him. Chico bore the full brunt of Groucho's black wit. But it never fazed him for long.

Groucho and Harpo almost always got along with each other. If there were any serious differences between the two, Daddy would act as a buffer. In fact, his role in the family was practically an extension of his place in the act: The two brothers channeled their remarks through him. Also, Groucho never had any reasons to be angry with Harpo. First, Groucho never had to worry about ever having to support him—Harpo died a wealthy man; and second, their styles of comedy were at different poles—the mime operated on another level from the madcap punster and raconteur.

On the other hand, Chico made Groucho feel insecure. In films, Chico's humor was much closer to Groucho's, and in real life his carefree attitude irked his brother. At the bottom

160

of it all was the fact that Chico had been Minnie's pet, although he hadn't tried to be.

But fights with Chico were brief; there was never any sustained animosity. Groucho yelled at Chico for losing at gambling, but just as regularly bailed Chico out. For his part, Chico didn't make an issue of Groucho's predominance in the act—if Groucho wanted the best lines, fine. Chico always put the act first.

That the brothers loved each other more than they did any collection of wives, daughters, or sons is hard for me to admit, but I think it was the case. The strength of their devotion to one another was tested year after year, and it never weakened. A day hardly passed that Daddy didn't hear from both brothers.

I realized that if I told Chico about Groucho's insulting remarks, he would have been angry with him—for about five minutes. Groucho would have just laughed it off.

Perhaps because of Groucho's rejection, I threw myself into getting a job. I would never give anyone an excuse to call me a parasite again! Or at least not a *lazy* parasite.

David O. Selznick had planned to present Ingrid Bergman in a Los Angeles stage production of *Anna Christie*, but switched it to the Lobero Theater in Santa Barbara because it supposedly had a more appreciative audience. With Chico's pull, I got a job there for the summer as a "gofer." In the second production of the season, I was given a bit part.

The play was *Lottie Dundas* by Enid Bagnold. It starred Geraldine Fitzgerald and Dame Mae Witty. I became friends with Dame Mae and her ancient but equally lovable husband, Ben Webster.

Uncle Ben, as he asked me to call him, had been a barrister in London when he had met Dame Mae, a chorus girl.

He asked her to marry him, but she replied that she wasn't going to give up the theater. So he decided to quit his practice and join her as an actor. Seven years later, they married.

I found it easy to open up to Dame Mae and tell her how confused and unhappy I was.

"I don't have the drive that my father has," I told her. "He's always pushing, making new plans. I don't have his self-assurance."

"I know it's tough when you have a star in the family," she said, "and you have four of them. My own daughter, Peggy, (Margaret Webster, the famous Shakespearean director) wanted to be in the business, and Ben and I had to push her very hard. It took some time, but now she's made it."

Dame Mae helped me gain perspective. It was a relief to hear that other people had doubts, too. I had always felt that because I had had such a strange childhood, my problems were also unique.

I had been seeing an endocrinologist to help me lose weight, but without success. One day, Dame Mae tactfully broached the subject of psychoanalysis to Mother.

My mother's reaction was immediate and predictable. "What do you mean? Do you think my daughter is crazy?"

After Mother had discussed it with a few other friends, she began to accept the idea.

"If you think it will help you, honey, then it's okay with me," she told me.

In those days, seeing a psychiatrist was almost an admission of being mentally ill. It took a great deal of understanding and plain guts for my mother to make the offer. To her, it was just some high-priced mumbo jumbo. But then she was scared at how quickly I had almost ruined my looks by overeating, and she was troubled by my depression. I didn't know what to think—I just wanted help.

I began to see an analyst five times a week. Almost the first question he asked was what I did for a living.

"I'm an actress."

162

"Are you making a living at it?"

"Well, no, but—"

"Then you can't claim to be an actress, can you?"

That settled, we soon got down to attacking my problems. Why was I perpetually late for appointments? Who did I think I was? Was my time more valuable than the time of those I kept waiting? These of course were manifestations of deeper matters.

Progress was slow, but I was beginning to feel almost human again. The pounds dropped off. I started to feel more courageous about asserting myself.

I found small parts opening up for me on the radio, without Daddy's help. I would still race to rehearsal, arriving in the nick of time, but I was working. I knew I could do better, even in radio, if I were slimmer. I had seen how male casting directors would hire actresses who weren't as good as I was, but who were more slender.

A woman director gave me my first leading role in *Sherlock Holmes*, starring Basil Rathbone. Holmes was put into a modern setting, and I played an Austrian girl trying to rescue her brother from a Nazi concentration camp. I must have been convincing, because my performance rated one of Groucho's rare compliments. I was back in his good graces.

Other parts, using other accents, followed. I was considered a find by casting directors because I could double as an American and a foreign girl in the same script. My ability to do a Bronx accent landed me a job in Norman Corwin's popular series, *Tales of Manhattan*. The show had originally been broadcast from New York, with Martin Gabel as the narrator. When it moved out to California, Orson Welles was recruited for the role. Corwin, an erudite man, tended to be a little pompous in rehearsals. Corwin would single out a word in the script, debating whether it was the proper one. Welles let this go on for a few times, and then started breaking the word down etymologically, usually citing its Greek roots.

As a radio actress, I became a known and reliable

quantity. I knew things were definitely improving when the question of my career again came up on the couch. This time, however, my analyst's comment made me feel as I had come a long way.

"You're acting, aren't you?" he said.

One afternoon, I ran into Ronald Colman in the CBS commissary. I had done a small part with him in the past, but I was sure he wouldn't recognize me.

"Good afternoon, Mr. Colman," I said, as he sat down next to me.

His eyes lit up. "Maxine Marx, right? I just went out with your Uncle Harpo. Had a wonderful time. Square dancing."

I was an occasional actress, but always a Marx.

"Maxine, dear, don't believe any of those stories you hear about me gambling. I have not played a game of gin rummy for over five dollars. . . . This is the absolute truth!" How many of my father's letters began or ended that way? After his band broke up in 1940 and he started travelling alone (though sometimes with Mary), usually sick and on a shoestring budget, I would receive his assurances that he was being "good" about gambling. But I knew that throughout his USO tours and, after the war, his European and American tours—mostly joke-deadening one-night stands—he continued to fly in the face of common sense.

I loved him for his ability to laugh off troubles that would have made most people bitter. Talking to a London journalist, Chico looked ahead to a month-long British tour: "Groucho and Harpo are rich men—but me, I'm in England." I was worried about his grueling schedule and sympathetic about his financial difficulties, but I refused to play what had been my mother's role. I didn't want to be my father's keeper. I was landing solid roles in leading radio shows without Chico's help, and soon I would be fully self-supporting. Of course, it was tough getting used to no longer being a millionaire's daughter, but after two years in analysis, I was able to face the prospect of having to work without coming apart.

Oddly enough, it was a silly practical joke that proved to be the event that propelled me out from under the domination of my family. Janet Cantor promised to babysit for her sister Natalie's children one September night in 1945. Sunny, a girl friend of ours, and I agreed to keep her company. As the evening wore on and the children dropped off to sleep, the three of us became bored with sitting around.

Janet hit on an idea. "Let's play a telephone joke on somebody."

I knew that I would be the one recruited, since I was able to do accents. None of us could stand George Jessel. We decided to pull his leg a bit. I would pretend to be a French acquaintance of his and make a date with him for later in the evening. Then I would stand him up. His phone number wasn't in Natalie's book, however, and it looked as if we would have to face a long dull night.

"Wait a minute," Sunny said. "There's a cute guy who comes into the bank." Sunny was a teller. "He just came back from a trip to Mexico. I know, because I changed some of his currency. His name is Jimmy Culhane."

"Is he married?" I asked.

"He's separated," Sunny said. "They just divided up their bank account."

"Good," I told her. "I don't want to get a married man in trouble."

We nervously dialed his number. "Allo, Jeemy," I said when he answered the phone, "deed I wake you?"

"Huh? Oh, no . . . no, not at all." He sounded groggy. "I was just reading."

"You don't remembaire me, do you?" I tried to keep my voice low and serious.

"It's coming back to me . . . "

"We met at a party in ze Valley. You tol' me you were going to Mexeeco and I said I would call you when you get back."

166

"I'm *so* glad you did!" Jimmy said.

We chatted and he asked me when he could see me. I was a little nervous about having to keep up the French girl routine, but I really liked talking with him. I thought of a place where I wouldn't run into any friends of my parents.

"'Ow about Sugies Tropics on Beverly Drive?"

"That's fine. Let's meet for dinner."

"No, no. Let's meet for dreenks, because I am not sure you really remembaire me and we may not want to stay for dinaire."

The day we agreed upon rolled around and Sunny went with me to the Tropics. She went in, spotted Jimmy, and came out to tell me what he was wearing and where he was sitting. I went in walked over to his seat and said, "Allo, Jeemy."

Jimmy later told me that he knew right away he had never set eyes on me before. We stayed at the bar for a while and since I didn't drink he suggested dinner. We sat at a table, and now I was faced with a dilemma. I had to protect the French bit, but what if we ran into Jimmy's friends and one of them spoke French. My French was good but hardly native.

So I told him I wouldn't speak French to anyone, until my English was perfect.

Sunny had said that Jimmy was in the animation field. At that time, Walt Disney's animators were on strike. I didn't want to become attracted to a "scab." To my relief, Jimmy said he was a director at the Walter Lantz Studio, which wasn't on strike.

There was one final problem. I realized that he wasn't Jewish, and I had to let him know that I was. Sticking as close to the truth as I could under the circumstances, I explained that my father was *un grand artiste* and we had fled "Eetler" as we were *juives*.

Jimmy seemed entranced by my French accent and corrected my English very gently all evening. He even told me that he much preferred European women and it never bothered him a bit about my being a Jew. The longer the evening went on, the less I felt the "joke" was funny. I became worried. I really liked Jimmy. How could I tell him the truth?

Finally, as we were about to leave, he asked me when he could see me again.

"Well," I told him, "I 'ave to tell you sometheeng that might change your mind."

"Don't tell me then."

"But I must if you want to see me again."

"Well, go ahead."

I took a deep breath and said without a trace of accent, "I really don't have to talk like that at all."

He looked at me for a full minute in disbelief. Then he started to laugh.

Every time he thought of something he had said against American women, and of how he had helped me with my English, he laughed even harder. He laughed until there were tears in his blue eyes, and I guess I fell in love with him right there and then.

Daddy was greatly amused when Shamus (that was Jimmy's nickname, Gaelic for James), and I offered to drop him off at Pickfair. Chico was going to perform at some benefit there, and his own car was out of whack. Shamus opened the door to let us into his 1939 Plymouth two-seater. Daddy and I jumped in and Chico immediately cracked up. The bumper was held together by bailing wire and the interior was in shreds. There was just enough room for three to squeeze in. Chico couldn't wait to drive up to the fancy mansion in Shamus' heap.

Chico was pleased that I was seriously involved with a man. Not that he and Shamus always hit it off. Daddy was sure his Irish jokes would go over big. "If I hear another Pat and Mike story," Shamus told me after one night out with Chico and Mary, "I'm going to throw something at your father."

Betty had doubts about Shamus, who was twice divorced.

"How do you know he'll settle down?" she asked me.

"He loves me, Mother, that's how I know."

She eventually fell in love with him, too. He was hard to resist. He was bright, gentle, and had a great sense of humor.

When Shamus and I decided to get married, Mother's wedding present was extravagant: a completely furnished house in Studio City. All of my uncles—except Zeppo, who was out of town—came for the ceremony.

When Chico arrived without Mary, I was relieved because Mother would never have stood for that. I could see them watching each other covertly all evening, and finally I made Betty go over to him.

"Betty, you look beautiful!" Chico exclaimed as if he had never seen her in a long dress before.

There was an awkward pause when Shamus came over.

"Well, Chico," Betty said in a low voice, "I think we both should drink a toast to the newlyweds." When their eyes met over the champagne glasses, Chico winked at her.

I suppose he was remembering their own mixed-up wedding plans, when the rabbi threw them out because Betty giggled. Those days must have seemed so far-off now.

Early in 1947 Chico suffered a heart attack while performing in Las Vegas. He was sixty, claiming to be fifty-five. I met Mary coming out of his hospital room.

"They say he's going to be fine—if he takes it easy," she told me.

"I don't think he'll ever take it easy."

"He will if I make him!" Mary said passionately. For a moment I was surprised at the degree of her emotion. I had always thought in the back of my mind that Mary, beautiful and half Chico's age, stayed around him because he was a star. But I could see that he had charmed her too—she was as hooked on the man as the rest of us were.

169

Mary was as good as her word. Chico decided it was the right time to retire from the public eye, and he and Mary, wife in all but name, settled down in Hollywood.

Daddy's retirement lasted two years. It wasn't the smell of the greasepaint that drew him back. He was strapped for money and had to work to make ends meet.

Chico persuaded Harpo, who really didn't need the money, to join him in an act consisting of bits and pieces from their pictures and ending with a piano and harp routine. They would play a few spots a year, usually Reno, Vegas, and Miami. It was a marvelously funny act, but a strenuous life for the brothers—especially for Daddy, who couldn't resist gambling at the resorts. Mary had no luck curbing him there.

Few people would have believed that the man they saw sliding across the stage on the seat of his pants, and gambling till all hours of the night, had a damaged heart. Harpo tried to discourage his older brother's self-destructive ways, but he refused to get too involved.

"I can't talk sense to your father. He just laughs at me, or worse, agrees to lay off the wild nights and then goes ahead and does what he wants to do. I can't control him, Maxine, and I don't want to hear about it anymore."

Harpo looked disgusted. I knew he wasn't kidding, either. Susan, Harpo's wife, had been trying for years to get him to stop worrying about Chico. She felt, probably rightly, that the act was ruining Harpo's health.

Groucho's career was better than ever. Since the brothers had broken up, Groucho had become popular on radio and later on TV. He too had distanced himself from his brother's plight.

Harpo and Daddy were still sublime, though, on stage. Both in their sixties, they managed to radiate a wonderful zest for life. They were stars from the twenties and thirties who never relied on nostalgia for a laugh.

LONDON, June 20–Harpo and Chico Marx, with their special brand of playing the harp and the fool, completely won a first-night audience at the Palladium tonight.

170

> *What makes these great clowns is a combination
> of fun and fantasy with something else, a mixture of
> worldly wisdom and naivete, of experience but also
> of an innocence never altogether lost, of dignity and
> absurdity together, so that for a moment we love
> and applaud mankind.*

As the star of a weekly ABC television show in which
he was cast as the proprietor of a soda fountain on a college
campus, Chico didn't fare as well. *The New York Times* turned
thumbs down on the show's premiere:

> *Chico has nothing to do . . . but practice his Italian
> dialect. He was at the keyboard for only a few bars,
> which is a prodigious waste of talent. . . . Chico
> deserves better fate than he is likely to get on "The
> College Bowl."*

It didn't help his situation any to find out that the
government was asking him for $70,000 in back taxes. Nor
did it improve his professional standing when *TV Guide*
reported that he had been forced to accept only $1,000 for a
role in "Playhouse 90." The public liked to hear about this
rags to riches back to rags again comedian, and wherever
Daddy performed, reporters always tried to get his reaction to
his changes in fortune. Daddy usually provided them with a
good gag. To James Thomas of the *London Express* he gave an
ironic summary of his financial woes:

> *I guess I lost around two million dollars gambling. I
> had money. I lost it—Las Vegas, the races, women.*
> *. . . The first crap game I played I lost $47,000 in
> one night. But I learned as I went along. In time I
> was able to lose more than that.*

Chico's health continued to fail. Early in 1959, he
toured in *The Fifth Season*. Not only was this the first time he
had acted in a role without his brothers, but it was the first
time he was without his Italian character. He was charming
and endearing on stage, and the audiences loved him. I went to

171

see the show in Boston and was deeply moved, watching Chico in his late sixties taking such a chance and pulling it off.

After each performance, he had to lie down. And he amazed the other performers: Before going on some nights, he would be so out of it that he'd ask any actor standing near him to "give me my first line and point me in the right direction." Then he'd amble on stage.

After the play closed, Chico went to England for a one-week concert tour. Recurring attacks of nausea forced him to cancel the engagement and return with Mary to Los Angeles.

In the last few years of his life, Chico and I talked every week on the phone. He would tell me new jokes, make light of his illness, and swap trivia. Then I would ask, "How's Uncle Groucho and Uncle Harpo?" Every week the answer would vary, depending on which brother had scolded him or had refused to do something he wanted done. One week he would say, "Groucho is a son of a bitch, but Harpo is the best brother a man could have!" The following week, the roles would be reversed.

One time when Daddy was berating Groucho as an unfeeling, lowdown bum, I said, "But Pop, remember what you told me, about Grandma never really showing him any affection and always preferring you, or Harpo, or even Gummo, but never Groucho?"

Daddy thought about it. "Yeah, you know Mom always called him 'the jealous one.' "

"Well," I said, "you can see why he gets angry at you at times and says more than he means. In some ways, he's still jealous."

"You may be right, honey. I never realized it before, but he was always trying to be the good son, while I was busy being the bad one—and yet Minnie always forgave me and loved me and was never that way with Grouch." Daddy was silent a moment. "I bet that explains a lot of things. . . . " After a few more jokes, love and kisses, he hung up. I knew he would promptly forget the "revelations" about Groucho's psychology. It wasn't in Chico to take such abstract things into consideration for long. Besides, next week Grouch was "the best brother a man could have, but Harpo . . ."

172

It was a rainy day, May 1961.

Harpo and I were riding up to the third floor of the Cedars of Lebanon hospital. We were both silent, full of dread. Chico had been hospitalized for what some Hollywood press agent euphemistically called "chest congestion." We knew differently: It was his second heart attack.

Groucho was in Dad's room when we got there. He was seated beside the gaunt, obviously stricken figure of Chico, lying propped up in bed.

As we came in, the atmosphere lightened. Daddy smiled when I kissed him. Harpo bent down and gave him a hug.

"Here are your cards," Harpo said, tossing the deck on the bed. "Now all you have to do is find the action."

"I think that nurse of yours has some action left," Groucho broke in, lifting his eyebrow.

"I wouldn't know about that . . ."

We all laughed. Chico's face lost ten years.

"Say Harp, Groucho and I were trying to remember that guy's name, the one who had the old abandoned warehouse when we were playing in *Animal Crackers*. You know . . . ?"

"Charlie," Harpo said, chuckling. "Fat Charlie."

"That's it. Maxine, I don't think you know this story." I shook my head. Daddy continued, "Well, when we were on Broadway with *Animal Crackers*, Zeppo had this friend who was crazy. Nuts. He was about five, two, and weighed maybe three hundred pounds."

"He walked on his heels and his eyes bulged," Harpo said, walking across the room with his "get tough" face.

"Right," Groucho took over the narrative. "This was during the days of Prohibition and everybody was after places where you could get booze. This character Charlie loved practical jokes, and he and Zeppo cooked up a great one which we'd pull on our friends."

"Only the best for our friends," Daddy winked.

"Anyway," Groucho went on, "after a show we'd

mention casually to a pal that we knew this guy downtown who had a warehouse where he had some good liquor fresh off the boat."

"Remember, we pulled this on Benny Leonard," Chico said.

"You mean the prizefighter?" I asked.

"Yeah. We told Benny about this guy and right away he's after us to bring him down and introduce him to our friend with the booze." Groucho said, pausing to light his cigar.

Harpo took over. "So we all piled into Zeppo's jalopy and off we go on this foggy night, all the way downtown to Charlie's warehouse. Charlie was waiting for us (Zeppo had called him from the theater so he was prepared), and did he look looney! While Fat Charlie's unlocking this huge warehouse door, I pulled Benny Leonard over to the side and whispered 'Now Benny, do whatever this guy tells you to. He's not quite right in the head. Just play along with him and you'll get all the booze we can carry.' Benny takes in the dark deserted street, the dark warehouse, and Fat Charlie, and mutters 'Sure, sure.' "

Chico interrupted his brother. "When we get inside, Charlie says, 'Before you get the stuff,' he points to Benny, 'let me see you dance.' Then Charlie starts playing an imaginary fiddle. 'Dance! I said, dance!' One of us nudges Benny, 'Better do as the man says.' So Benny Leonard, one of the all-time great boxers, a guy who'd walk into the ring for a fight and tell his opponent not to mess his hair or he'd kill him, this man starts to dance!"

The brothers broke up.

Groucho continued the story. "After the dance, when Fat Charlie turned his back on us for a minute, we yelled to Benny, 'Let's get out of here!' and took off for the car. When we made it inside the car, Benny was pale and just wrecked. He looked out the window and saw Fat Charlie come wobbling along on his heels, thrashing his arms, and waving some chains that were around his neck.

174

" 'Let's go, you guys! Come on!' Benny screamed.

"Zeppo in the driver's seat mumbles something about not knowing where the keys are, and then, just before Benny goes nuts, finds the key and we drive off.'"

"I'm glad I wasn't there when you told him it was a joke," I said.

"Oh, Benny was a swell guy. Great sense of humor," Daddy said.

"What your father means is that we hid from Benny for two weeks after that night, until a friend of his told us it was all right to come out," Groucho said.

When Harpo, Groucho, and I left Chico, he was still in high spirits, his face reflecting the glow of better days.

Shortly afterwards, Daddy was moved home to Mary. I saw him one more time.

I kissed him hello. He was quiet a moment. Then he said, "I wish I were Groucho so I could help you out."

I looked into his eyes. "I wouldn't exchange you for anybody."

His nurse came in. "Mr. Marx, is it time for us to brush our teeth?"

"Later, nurse," he said.

She left the room.

"Is it time to brush our teeth?" he mimicked. "Is it time to drink our juice? Who does she think we are, anyway?"

He still hadn't lost his sense of humor.

Before I left that day, Chico said, "Remember, honey, don't forget what I told you. Put in my coffin a deck of cards, a mashie niblick, and a pretty blonde."

I nodded and left the room in tears.

Chico died October 11, 1961.

The funeral services were held two days later, at the Wee Kirk O' the Heather Chapel at Forest Lawn Memorial Park in Los Angeles, on Friday the thirteenth.

Knowing how Daddy had reacted to deaths in the family, I expected his brothers not to show too much emotion at his passing. They didn't surprise me. As I was getting out of

175

the limousine with Groucho, he offered me some consolation: "Well, at least it's SRO," he said, indicating the packed group of spectators standing in the back of the chapel, most of whom were stargazers. Some of Daddy's old friends were there as well: Jimmy Durante, George Burns, and Buster Keaton. Daddy would have been pleased.

Unfortunately, Mary had insisted on a religious ceremony, despite Chico's lack of interest in religion, and Gummo had dutifully brought in a rabbi to officiate. The rabbi, I'm positive, had never known Daddy for a minute. I went over to him and asked him to do me a favor. "The only thing that I'd like you to say is that Chico Marx was the least *malicious* man who ever lived." He nodded his head. That he could do.

During the service, his voice droned on. His eulogy for Chico was completely off the mark. Nothing rang true. I looked at Groucho and Harpo, and they were squirming with discomfort too.

"I have been asked by his daughter," the rabbi finally said, "to say that her father was the least *mischievous* man in the world."

Groucho and I were angry.

"I should have delivered it myself," Groucho said with disgust.

"Listen," Harpo said to me, leaning over Groucho, "when I go, do me a favor and hire a mime."

When I walked out of the chapel, I noticed the ashen faces of Durante and Keaton. With Daddy dead, the Marx Brothers had started the ultimate fade into celluloid, and I saw that these old comics sensed this without having it put into words. A great age of comedy was passing, the age of the vaudevillians, the pioneers, the men who moved from the stage into the silent films and later to the talkies. The tears I saw in Keaton's eyes were for an era gone by.

176

The New York Times, in an editorial entitled, "An Echo of Lost Laughter," verbalized the look on Durante's face:

> *When the news of Chico Marx's death was published millions of Americans had to accept another disturbing fact. The Marx Brothers as a band of slapstick clowns will never play again. Excepting expert comic pantomime on television two years ago, called "The Incredible Jewel Robbery," and grossly unappreciated, they have been going their separate ways for years. Chico amused himself by leading a dance band orchestra.*
>
> *But while Groucho, Harpo and Chico were all available, there was always an outside chance that they might vandalize the land of cuckoo once more. To theatregoers and moviegoers it seemed simple enough. All Groucho had to do was paint on that moustache, clamp a cigar in his mouth, and walk with a stoop. All Harpo had to do was slap on the wig, toot the rubber horn and leer at girls. Chico had only to put on the pointed hat and short jacket and shoot the piano keys. Nothing looked simpler.*
>
> *It can never be. The funniest team of twentieth century mountebanks is broken, beyond repair . . . No more. Alas, poor Chico. Alas, ourselves.*

All true. But the tears in my eyes were for the man.

INDEX

179